Exerci:

THE
BRIEF HOLT
HANDBOOK

Second Edition

KIRSZNER & MANDELL

Exercises to accompany

THE
BRIEF HOLT
HANDBOOK

Second Edition

KIRSZNER & MANDELL

Prepared by

Scott Douglass
Chattanooga
State Technical
Community College

Peggy B. Jolly
University of
Alabama
at Birmingham

Judy A. Pearce
Montgomery
College

Harcourt Brace College Publishers

Fort Worth   Philadelphia   San Diego
New York   Orlando   Austin   San Antonio
Toronto   Montreal   London   Sydney   Tokyo

ISBN: 0-15-505357-4

Copyright © 1998, 1995 by Harcourt Brace & Company

All rights reserved. No part of this publication may be reproduced or transmitted in any form or by any means, electronic or mechanical, including photocopy, recording, or any information storage and retrieval system, without permission in writing from the publisher, except that, until further notice, the contents or parts thereof may be reproduced for instructional purposes by users of THE BRIEF HOLT HANDBOOK, Second Edition by Laurie G. Kirszner and Stephen R. Mandell.

Address editorial correspondence to:
Harcourt Brace College Publishers
301 Commerce Street, Suite 3700
Fort Worth, TX 76102

Address orders to:
Harcourt Brace & Company
6277 Sea Harbor Drive
Orlando, FL 32887
1-800-782-4479 outside Florida
1-800-433-0001 inside Florida

Printed in the United States of America

. 7 8 9 0 1 2 3 4 5 6   066   9 8 7 6 5 4 3 2 1

Contents

	Brief Exercises	Brief *Holt* Handbook

Writing Essays

EXERCISE 1: Getting Started 1 3

EXERCISE 2: Considering Purpose and Audience 2 4–6

EXERCISE 3: Listing 3 6–7

EXERCISE 4: Freewriting 4 8

EXERCISE 5: Brainstorming 5 8

EXERCISE 6: Journal Entry 6 10

EXERCISE 7: Cluster Diagram / Topic Tree 7 10–13

EXERCISE 8: Developing a Thesis 8 12

EXERCISE 9: Stating a Thesis 10 14

EXERCISE 10: Stating a Thesis 11 14

EXERCISE 11: Thesis 12 15

EXERCISE 12: Informal Outline 12 17

EXERCISE 13: Rough Draft 13 19

EXERCISE 14: Collaborative Revision 14 22

EXERCISE 15: Customized Checklist 16 23

Writing Paragraphs

EXERCISE 16: Central Idea—
Topic Sentence 17 36

EXERCISE 17: Coherence within
Paragraphs 19 37

EXERCISE 18: Coherence among
Paragraphs 21 37

EXERCISE 19: Patterns of Paragraph
Development 24 41

EXERCISE 20: Well-Developed
Paragraphs 25 47

Sentence Fragments

EXERCISE 21: Revising Sentence
Fragments 28 74

EXERCISE 22: Revising Sentence
Fragments 30 74

EXERCISE 23: Revising Sentence
Fragments 32 74

EXERCISE 24: Revising Sentence
Fragments 35 74

EXERCISE 25: Revising Sentence
Fragments 37 74

EXERCISE 26: Revising Sentence
Fragments 39 76

EXERCISE 27: Revising Sentence
Fragments 41 76

Comma Splices and Fused Sentences

EXERCISE 28: Revising Comma Splices and Fused Sentences 43 78

EXERCISE 29: Sentence Combining 45 80

Agreement

EXERCISE 30: Subject-Verb Agreement 48 82

EXERCISE 31: Subject-Verb Agreement 50 82

EXERCISE 32: Subject-Verb, Pronoun-Antecedent Agreement 52 87

EXERCISE 33: Subject-Verb, Pronoun-Antecedent Agreement 54 87

Verbs

EXERCISE 34: Principal Parts 57 90

EXERCISE 35: Principal Parts 58 90

EXERCISE 36: Tense 59 94

EXERCISE 37: Tense 62 94

EXERCISE 38: Mood 65 98

EXERCISE 39: Voice 66 100

EXERCISE 40: Voice 68 100

EXERCISE 41: Voice 70 100

Pronouns

EXERCISE 42: Pronoun Case 71 101

EXERCISE 43: Sentence Combining 73 101–104

EXERCISE 44: Pronoun Reference 75 104

Adjectives and Adverbs

EXERCISE 45: Modification 78 107

EXERCISE 46: Sentence Modeling 80 108–109

EXERCISE 47: Comparative and
Superlative Forms 81 109–110

EXERCISE 48: Nouns as Modifiers 84 110

Sentence Variety

EXERCISE 49: Combining for Variety 86 115

EXERCISE 50: Combining for Variety 88 116

EXERCISE 51: Revising for Variety 90 117–118

EXERCISE 52: Revising for Variety 93 119

EXERCISE 53: Opening Strategies 94 120

EXERCISE 54: Revising for Variety 97 121

Emphatic Sentences

EXERCISE 55: Revising for Emphasis 100 123

EXERCISE 56: Revising for Emphasis 102 126–127

EXERCISE 57: Active Voice for Emphasis 105 127

Concise Sentences

EXERCISE 58: Revising for Conciseness 107 129–131

EXERCISE 59: Revising for Conciseness 109 132

EXERCISE 60: Revising for Conciseness 111 133–135

Awkward or Confusing Sentences

EXERCISE 61: Shifts in Tense, Voice, Mood, Person, Number 113 136–138

EXERCISE 62: Shifts from Direct to Indirect Discourse 118 138

EXERCISE 63: Mixed Constructions 123 139

EXERCISE 64: Faulty Predication 125 140

EXERCISE 65: Incomplete or Illogical Comparisons 127 141

Parallelism

EXERCISE 66: Using Parallelism 129 143

EXERCISE 67: Sentence Combining 131 143

EXERCISE 68: Correcting Faulty
Parallelism 135 144

Modifiers

EXERCISE 69: Identifying Headwords ... 138 146

EXERCISE 70: Connecting Modifiers
and Headwords 140 146

EXERCISE 71: Relocating Misplaced
Modifiers 142 147

EXERCISE 72: Relocating Misplaced
Modifiers 144 147

EXERCISE 73: Eliminating Dangling
Modifiers 146 148–150

Effective Words

EXERCISE 74: Level of Diction 149 153

EXERCISE 75: General and Specific;
Abstract and Concrete 151 155–156

EXERCISE 76: Denotation and
Connotation 152 155–156

EXERCISE 77: Denotation and
Connotation 154 155–156

EXERCISE 78: Figures of Speech 155 158

EXERCISE 79: Figures of Speech 157 158

EXERCISE 80: Eliminating Biased
Language 159 159

EXERCISE 81: Gender-Neutral
Alternatives 161 159–161

EXERCISE 82: Terms Denoting
Professions 163 159–161

EXERCISE 83: Gender-Neutral
Coinages 164 159–161

EXERCISE 84: Masculine/Feminine
Word Forms 165 159–161

Using the Dictionary

EXERCISE 85: Grammatical Forms 166 163

EXERCISE 86: Usage Restrictions 167 164

EXERCISE 87: Research Capabilities 168 163

EXERCISE 88: Histories of Words 169 163

Punctuation

EXERCISE 89: Periods 170 189

EXERCISE 90: Question Marks 171 190

EXERCISE 91: Exclamation Points 172 191

EXERCISE 92: Review of End
Punctuation 173 189–192

Commas

EXERCISE 93: Commas in Compound
Sentences 174 193

xi

EXERCISE 94: Commas to Separate
                Items in a Series 176 194

EXERCISE 95: Commas to Separate
                Coordinate Adjectives 177 195

EXERCISE 96: Commas to Set Off
                Introductory Elements 178 196

EXERCISE 97: Commas to Set Off
                Nonrestrictive Elements .. 180 197

EXERCISE 98: Commas to Set Off
                Nonessential Elements 181 197

EXERCISE 99: Commas to Set Off
                Quotations, Names,
                Dates, Etc. 183 201–202

EXERCISE 100: Commas to Prevent
                Misreading 185 202

EXERCISE 101: Review of Commas 186 193–205

Semicolons

EXERCISE 102: Punctuation to Separate
                Independent Clauses 188 206

EXERCISE 103: Semicolons to Separate
                Independent Clauses 191 206

EXERCISE 104: Sentence Combining 193 207

EXERCISE 105: Semicolons to Separate
                Items in a Series 195 207

EXERCISE 106: Sentence Combining 197 207

EXERCISE 107: Review of
                Semicolons 200 206–208

Apostrophes

EXERCISE 108: Possessives 202 209

EXERCISE 109: Possessives 203 209

EXERCISE 110: Plural Nouns or
                Possessive Pronouns 204 209–210

EXERCISE 111: Contractions 206 211

EXERCISE 112: Plurals of Letters
                and Numbers 208 212

Quotation Marks

EXERCISE 113: Direct Quotations 209 213

EXERCISE 114: Titles and Words Used
                in a Special Sense 210 214–215

EXERCISE 115: Dialogue 211 215

EXERCISE 116: Review of
                Quotation Marks 212 213–219

EXERCISE 117: Review of
                Quotation Marks 214 213–219

Other Punctuation Marks

EXERCISE 118: Colons 216 220

EXERCISE 119: Dashes 217 222

EXERCISE 120: Parentheses 218 223

EXERCISE 121: Ellipses 219 225

EXERCISE 122: Review of Colons,
Dashes, Parentheses,
Brackets, Slashes 221 220–227

Spelling and Mechanics

EXERCISE 123: *ie* or *ei* 223 223

EXERCISE 124: Suffixes 224 224

EXERCISE 125: Final *y* 225 224

EXERCISE 126: Capitalization 226 237–241

EXERCISE 127: Italics 229 242–244

EXERCISE 128: Hyphens 231 245

EXERCISE 129: Hyphens 232 246

EXERCISE 130: Hyphens 233 246

EXERCISE 131: Abbreviations 235 249–252

EXERCISE 132: Numbers 238 253–255

Research

EXERCISE 133: Time Management 241 259

EXERCISE 134: Discovering Your
Research Question 242 261

EXERCISE 135: Exploring Your Topic
 and Locating Sources 244 259–269

EXERCISE 136: Evaluating Sources 245 285

EXERCISE 137: Locating and Evaluating
 Sources on the Web
 Using URL's 246 276

EXERCISE 138: Locating and Evaluating
 Sources on the Web
 Using a Key
 Word Search 247 276–279

EXERCISE 139: Doing Your Own Key
 Word Search 248 276–279

EXERCISE 140: Citing Electronic
 Sources 249 320–323

EXERCISE 141: Summarizing 250 289

EXERCISE 142: Paraphrasing 252 290

EXERCISE 143: Quoting 252 291

EXERCISE 144: Documentation 253 309–342

Note to Students

Many of these exercises direct you to "write your changes between the lines" so that you need not recopy whole sentences or paragraphs. Ask your instructor how you should indicate deletions and insertions in these exercises. Or, your instructor may have reasons for wanting you to recopy these exercises on a separate piece of paper. Find out what your instructor's preferences are before you begin.

Page references in these exercises refer to the second edition of *The* Brief *Holt Handbook* (1998) by Kirszner and Mandell.

NAME _____ DATE _____ SCORE _____

EXERCISE 1: Getting Started

Take as your general subject a book that you liked or disliked very much.

1. How would each of the following writing situations affect the content, style, organization, tone, and emphasis of an essay about this book?

    - A journal entry recording your informal impressions of the book

    - An examination question that asks you to summarize the book's main idea

    - A book review for a composition class in which you evaluate both the book's strengths and its weaknesses

    - A letter to your local school board in which you try to convince your readers that, regardless of the book's style or content, it should not be banned from the local public library

    - An editorial for your school newspaper in which you try to persuade other students that the book is not worth reading

2. Choose one of the writing situations listed in number 1, and write an opening paragraph for the specified assignment. Continue on plain paper if you need more space.

NAME _____ DATE _____ SCORE _____

EXERCISE 2: Considering Purpose and Audience

Consider an essay subject you have chosen or your instructor has assigned. How will your purpose and audience affect what you write and how you write?

1. Name your subject.

2. What is your purpose?

3. Who is your audience?

4. What will you write and how will you write?

5. Write your first paragraph below. Continue on plain paper if you need more space.

NAME _____ DATE _____ SCORE _____

EXERCISE 3: Listing

List all the sources you encounter in one day (people, books, magazines, observations, and so on) that could provide you with useful information for the essay you are writing.

NAME _____ DATE _____ SCORE _____

EXERCISE 4: Freewriting

Begin with the most important sentence or idea from the paragraph you wrote in Exercise 2. Freewrite until you have filled this page. Continue to freewrite on your own paper if you can.

NAME _____ DATE _____ SCORE _____

EXERCISE 5: Brainstorming

Consider what you have discovered in Exercises 2–4. Do you need to change any part of your plan for your essay?

1. What is your subject?

2. What is your purpose?

3. Who is your audience?

4. List all the points you can think of that seem pertinent to your essay.

Copyright © 1998 by Harcourt Brace & Company. All rights reserved.

NAME _____ DATE _____ SCORE _____

EXERCISE 6: Journal Entry

Write a journal entry evaluating your progress so far. Which of the strategies for finding something to say worked best for you? Why?

NAME _____ DATE _____ SCORE _____

EXERCISE 7: Cluster Diagram/Topic Tree

Reread the work you did for Exercises 2–6. Use this material to help you construct a cluster diagram or a topic tree. This exercise should help you to see how the ideas you have discovered can be organized into related groups.

NAME _____ DATE _____ SCORE _____

EXERCISE 8: Developing a Thesis

Analyze the following statements or topics and explain why none of them qualifies as an effective thesis. Be prepared to explain how each could be improved.

1. In this essay, I will examine the environmental effects of residential and commercial development on the coastal regions of the United States.

2. Residential and commercial development in the coastal regions of the United States

3. How to avoid coastal overdevelopment

4. Coastal development: pro and con

5. Residential and commercial development of America's coastal regions benefits some people, but it has some disadvantages.

6. The environmentalists' position on coastal development

7. More and more coastal regions in the United States are being overdeveloped.

NAME _____ DATE _____ SCORE _____

8. Residential and commercial development guidelines need to be developed for coastal regions of the United States.

9. Coastal development is causing beach erosion.

10. At one time I enjoyed walking on the beach, but commercial and residential development has ruined the experience for me.

NAME _____ DATE _____ SCORE _____

EXERCISE 9: Stating a Thesis

Formulate a clearly worded thesis statement for the following topics.

1. A person who has profoundly influenced the course of your life

2. Gun control and the Second Amendment

3. Should medical use of marijuana be made lawful?

4. Preparing for your retirement

5. The value of a college education

6. Public funding of the arts

7. Shoplifting

8. The role of cultural diversity

9. Parochial vs. secular education

10. Political correctness and the First Amendment

NAME _____ DATE _____ SCORE _____

EXERCISE 10: Stating a Thesis

Read the following sentences excerpted from the essay "Territoriality and Dominance" by René Dubos. Then develop a thesis that will tie together the information in the sentences. Make sure your thesis is well constructed and follows the requirements outlined in this chapter.

- Whenever the population density of a group increases beyond a safe limit, many of the low-ranking animals in the social hierarchy are removed from the reproductive pool.

- The remarkable outcome of these automatic mechanisms is that, in the case of many animal species, animal populations in the wild remain on the average much more stable than would be expected from the maximum reproductive potential.

- When males fight, the combat is rarely to the death.

- The losing animal in a struggle saves itself . . . by an act of submission, an act usually recognized and accepted by the winner.

- The view that destructive combat is rare among wild animals . . . is at variance with the "Nature, red in tooth and claw" legend.

- Since ritualization of behavior is widespread among the higher apes, it is surprising that humans differ from them, as well as from most other animals, in practicing warfare extensively with the intent to kill.

NAME _____ DATE _____ SCORE _____

EXERCISE 11: Thesis

Review the cluster diagram or the topic tree you made in Exercise 7. Use it to help you to develop a thesis for an essay you are working on. Write your thesis in the space below.

EXERCISE 12: Informal Outline

After reviewing your notes, prepare an informal outline for a paper on the thesis you developed in Exercise 11.

NAME _____ DATE _____ SCORE _____

EXERCISE 13: Rough Draft

Write a rough draft of the essay you have been planning. Continue on your own paper if you need more space.

NAME _____ DATE _____ SCORE _____

EXERCISE 14: Collaborative Revision

After you have drafted a paper, form teams of two or three for collaborative revision. Read each other's papers and write responses to the "Questions for Collaborative Revision" below. Then discuss the comments. You may be asked to work with the same team for each assignment or to change teams each time.

- What is the essay about? Is the topic suitable for this assignment?

- What is the main point of the essay? Is the thesis stated? If so, is it clearly worded? If not, how can the wording be improved? Is the thesis stated in an appropriate place?

- Is the essay arranged logically? Do the body paragraphs appear in an appropriate order?

- What ideas support the thesis? Does each body paragraph develop one of these?

- Does each body paragraph have a unifying idea? Are topic sentences needed to summarize the information in the paragraphs? Are the topic sentences clearly related to the thesis?

NAME _____ DATE _____ SCORE _____

- Is any necessary information missing? Identify any areas that seem to need further development. Is any information irrelevant? If so, indicate possible deletions.

- Can you contribute anything to the essay? Can you think of any ideas or examples from your own reading, experience, or observations that would strengthen the writer's points?

- Can you follow the writer's ideas? If not, would clearer connections between sentences or paragraphs be helpful? If so, where are such connections needed?

- Is the introductory paragraph interesting to you? Would another kind of introduction work better?

- Does the conclusion leave you with a sense of completion? Would another kind of conclusion be more appropriate?

- Is anything unclear or confusing?

- What is the essay's greatest strength?

- What is the essay's greatest weakness?

Copyright © 1998 by Harcourt Brace & Company. All rights reserved.

NAME _____ DATE _____ SCORE _____

EXERCISE 15: Customized Checklist

Using the revision checklists on pp. 23–25 of *The* Brief *Holt Handbook* as a guide, create a customized checklist—one that reflects the specific concerns you need to consider to revise your essay—in the space below. Then revise your essay according to this checklist.

After revising, edit your essay and then prepare a final draft, being sure to proofread it carefully.

NAME _____ DATE _____ SCORE _____

EXERCISE 16: Central Idea—Topic Sentence

Each of the following paragraphs is unified by a central idea, but that idea is not explicitly stated. Identify the unifying idea of each paragraph, write a topic sentence that expresses it, and indicate with a caret (^) where the topic sentence should be placed in the paragraph.

A. The narrator in Ellison's novel leaves an all-black college in the South to seek his fortune—and his identity—in the North. Throughout the story he experiences bigotry in all forms. Blacks as well as whites, friends as well as enemies, treat him according to their preconceived notions of what he should be, or how he can help to advance their causes. Clearly this is a book about racial prejudice. However, on another level, *Invisible Man* is more than the account of a young African-American's initiation into the harsh realities of life in the United States before the civil rights movement. The narrator calls himself invisible because others refuse to see him. He becomes so alienated from society—black and white—that he chooses to live in isolation. But, when he has learned to see himself clearly, he will emerge demanding that others see him, too.

NAME _____ DATE _____ SCORE _____

B. "Lite" can mean a product has fewer calories, or less fat, or less sodium, or it can simply mean the product has a "light" color, texture, or taste. It may mean none of these. Food can be advertised as 86 percent fat free when it is actually 50 percent fat, because the term "fat free" is based on weight and fat is extremely light. Another misleading term is "no cholesterol," which is found on some products that never had any cholesterol in the first place. Peanut butter, for example, contains no cholesterol—a fact that manufacturers have recently made an issue—but it is very high in fat and so would not be a very good food for most dieters. Sodium labeling presents still another problem. The terms, "sodium free" "very low sodium," "low sodium," "reduced sodium," and "no salt added" have very specific meanings, frequently not explained on the packages on which they appear.

NAME _____ DATE _____ SCORE _____

EXERCISE 17: Coherence within Paragraphs

A. Read the following paragraph and determine how the author achieves coherence. Underline parallel elements, pronouns, repeated words, and transitional words and phrases that link sentences. Label these devices in the margins.

Some years ago the old elevated railway in Philadelphia was torn down and replaced by the subway system. This ancient El with its barnlike stations containing nut-vending machines and scattered food scraps had, for generations, been the favorite feeding ground of flocks of pigeons, generally one flock to a station along the route of the El. Hundreds of pigeons were dependent upon the system. They flapped in and out of its stanchions and steel work or gathered in watchful little audiences about the feet of anyone who rattled the peanut-vending machines. They even watched people who jingled change in their hands, and prospected for food under the feet of the crowds who gathered between trains. Probably very few among the waiting people who tossed a crumb to an eager pigeon realized

NAME _____ DATE _____ SCORE _____

that this El was like a food-bearing river, and that the life which haunted its banks was dependent upon the running of the trains with their human freight. (Loren Eiseley, *The Night Country*)

B. Supplying the missing transitional words and phrases, revise the following paragraph to make it coherent. Write your changes between the lines.

The theory of continental drift was first put forward by Alfred Wegener in 1912. The continents fit together like a gigantic jigsaw puzzle. The opposing Atlantic coasts, especially South America and Africa, seem to have been attached. He believed that at one time, probably 225 million years ago, there was one supercontinent. This continent broke into parts that drifted into their present positions. The theory stirred controversy during the 1920s and eventually was ridiculed by the scientific community. In 1954 the theory was revived. The theory of continental drift is accepted as a reasonable geological explanation of the continental system. (Student Writer)

EXERCISE 18: Coherence among Paragraphs

Read the following paragraph cluster. Then revise as necessary to increase coherence among paragraphs. Write your changes between the lines.

Leave It to Beaver and *Father Knows Best* were typical of the late 1950s and early 1960s. Both were popular during a time when middle-class mothers stayed home to raise their children while fathers went to "the office." The Beaver's mother, June Cleaver, always wore a dress and high heels, even when she vacuumed. So did Margaret Anderson, the mother on *Father Knows Best*. Wally and the Beaver lived a picture-perfect small-town life, and Betty, Bud, and Kathy never had a problem that father Jim Anderson couldn't solve.

The Brady Bunch featured six children and the typical Mom-at-home and Dad-at-work combination. Of course, Florence Brady did wear pants,

NAME _____ DATE _____ SCORE _____

and the Bradys were what today would be called a "blended family." Nevertheless, *The Brady Bunch* presented a hopelessly idealized picture of upper-middle-class suburban life. The Brady kids lived in a large split-level house, went on vacations, had two loving parents, and even had a live-in maid, the ever-faithful, wisecracking Alice. Everyone in town was heterosexual, employed, able-bodied, and white.

The Cosby Show was extremely popular. It featured two professional parents, a doctor and a lawyer. They lived in a townhouse with original art on the walls, and money never seemed to be a problem. In addition to warm relationships with their siblings, the Huxtable children also had close ties to their grandparents. *The Cosby Show* did introduce problems, such as son Theo's

NAME _____ DATE _____ SCORE _____

dyslexia, but in many ways it replicated the 1950s formula. Even in the 1990s, it seems, father still knows best.

NAME _____ DATE _____ SCORE _____

EXERCISE 19: Patterns of Paragraph Development

Determine one possible method of development for a paragraph on each of these topics. Then write a paragraph on one of the topics.

1. What an ideal date is (or is not)

2. How to write a paragraph

3. The types of people who go to concerts

4. A perfect day

5. Humanism vs. secularism

6. The connection between educational level and success

7. Technology and a changing society

8. Word processing and composition

9. Doctor-assisted suicide

10. Money's influence on sports

NAME _____ DATE _____ SCORE _____

EXERCISE 20: Well-Developed Paragraphs

A. Read each of the following paragraphs and then answer these questions. In general terms, how could each paragraph be developed further? What pattern of development might be used in each case?

B. Choose one paragraph. Rewrite it to develop it further. To assess the development of your revised paragraph, consult the checklist on pp. 48-49. *The Brief Holt Handbook*. Revise again if necessary.

   1. Civility once was considered the cornerstone of a progressive society. Disagreements were noted, but seldom publicly acknowledged. Violation of this custom among certain classes often resulted in the practice of dueling, which acted as a deterrent to uncivil behavior because of the finality of the outcome. Though dueling is now outlawed in our society, many disagreements are still settled through violence. The lack of civility remains problematic in our society.

   2. Amish Friendship Bread is a culinary treat. It begins with the receipt of a gift of a batch of starter batter. The entire process from receiving the batter to the finished product takes ten days. The first day requires the addition of flour, milk, and sugar. Days two through five involve the once-a-day, gentle mixing of the batter. On day six, more milk, flour, and sugar are added. Days seven through nine repeat the

NAME _____ DATE _____ SCORE _____

daily mixing. On day ten, the long anticipated outcome is realized as a portion of the batter is baked into a succulent loaf while saving a starter batch to share with a friend.

3. Conservatives and Liberals make up the extremes of our two mainstream political parties. The Great Silent Majority, those who hold a mixture of these views, constitutes the bulk of those who are politically active. Politicians are left with the difficult task of trying to appease the interests of all three groups.

4. Most people look forward to vacations with great eagerness. Where they vacation, however, differs widely. Vacation locations depend on such factors as personal preference, financial considerations, and time available. Some people look forward to spending a few days in the mountains while others can think of nothing more pleasant than sunning on a sugar-white beach. Regardless of their choices, vacations remain the goal and basis of fond memories for nearly everyone.

NAME _____ DATE _____ SCORE _____

5. Young adults are social creatures. They enjoy gathering with others their age to celebrate all types of occasions. For example, a football game may be preceded by an overnight tailgate party, or a group may gather for a clam bake on a beach, or spring break may demand a special celebration. No matter the type of gathering, attention must be paid to details in order to make the celebration memorable.

6. Personal views on certain issues such as capital punishment, abortion, and euthanasia are usually strongly stated. Views may be based on personal experience, religion, family, or societal beliefs. Discussing these views with others who disagree can result in heated debate and occasional enlightenment about why contrary opinions are held. The important thing to remember about these types of discussions is that they should be based on reason rather than emotion.

NAME _____ DATE _____ SCORE _____

EXERCISE 21: Revising Sentence Fragments

Identify the sentence fragments in the following paragraph and correct each one, either by attaching the fragment to an independent clause or by deleting the subordinating conjunction or relative pronoun to create a sentence that can stand alone. In some cases you will have to replace a relative pronoun with another word that can serve as the subject of an independent clause. Write your changes between the lines.

Muscle cars were introduced to Americans in the 1960s. When the price of gasoline was relatively inexpensive. The cars evolved from the earlier, less powerful stock versions. Such as the 1964 ½ Ford Mustang. That had a six-cylinder engine. Next came the 289 cc V-8 engine. The public's clamor for ever more powerful engines was answered by the industry's introduction of the 390 cc engine. Which ended in the Shelby Mustang GT variant with the awesome Cleveland Boss engine. Not to be outdone, General Motors introduced its Oldsmobile 442, Chevelle

NAME _____ DATE _____ SCORE _____

SS 396, and Camaro. Chrysler's Fury and Road Runner soon joined the pack. These cars, often featured in Hollywood film chase scenes such as that made famous by Steve McQueen in <u>Bullit</u>, were targeted at a youth market, late teenagers and young adults. Who often used the cars as a status symbol. Muscle cars could be seen lining the pits of drag races on Saturday nights and cruising the city's main streets and hamburger drive-ins on the weekend. Driving around mall parking lots in their thundering, glass-pack exhausted behemoths. Trying to impress the opposite sex. The popularity of the muscle car was brought down by the oil embargo of the 1970s. Which brought long lines at gasoline stations, fuel rationing, and increasing prices. The love affair with these cars, though, continues. If only as a form of nostalgia.

NAME _____ DATE _____ SCORE _____

EXERCISE 22: Revising Sentence Fragments

Read the following passage and identify the sentence fragments. Then correct each one by attaching it to the independent clause that contains the word or word group it modifies. Write your changes between the lines.

Most college athletes are caught in a conflict. Between their athletic and academic careers. Sometimes college athletes' responsibilities on the playing field make it hard for them to be good students. Often athletes must make a choice. Between sports and a degree. Some athletes would not be able to afford college. Without athletic scholarships. But, ironically, their commitments to sports (training, exercise, practice, and travel to out-of-town games, for example) deprive athletes. Of valuable classroom time. The role of college athletes is constantly being questioned. Critics suggest athletes exist only to participate in and promote college athletics. Because of the

NAME _____ DATE _____ SCORE _____

importance of this role to academic institutions, scandals occasionally develop. With coaches and even faculty members arranging to inflate athletes' grades to help them remain eligible. For participation in sports. Some universities even lower admissions standards. To help remedy this and other inequities. The controversial Proposition 48, passed at the NCAA convention in 1982, established minimum College Board scores and grade standards for college students. But many people feel that the NCAA remains overly concerned. With profits rather than with education. As a result, college athletic competition is increasingly coming to resemble pro sports. From the coaches' pressure on the players to win to the network television exposure to the wagers on the games' outcomes.

EXERCISE 23: Revising Sentence Fragments

Identify and correct the sentence fragments in the following paragraphs by attaching the fragment to a related independent clause or adding a subject and a verb to create a new independent clause. Write your changes between the lines.

CRASH. The year was 1929. The speculative boom in stocks that seemed unending came to a screeching halt in October. On the day that has come to be known as Black Monday. It caused an entire generation to distrust equities. At first, the far-reaching effects of the crash were not understood. Seeming to affect directly only those who owned stocks and bonds. Those who lost their entire fortune in one afternoon. Those financially devastated individuals who saw no alternative other than suicide. Leaping from the windows of tall buildings on Wall Street. Soon, though, the awful truth became apparent. The entire country

NAME _____ DATE _____ SCORE _____

slowly slid into economic despair known as the Great Depression. Which lasted for an entire decade. Companies went out of business, jobs were scarce, food lines began to form. Men left their families to ride the rails as hobos. Looking for any job they could find.

Until the federal government intervened. By creating the WPA, a program designed to build public works projects such as dams and roadways, to employ large numbers of people. The economic depression ended when the country entered World War II. When military production energized the flagging economy. True to the inherent nature of market cycles, the revived economy created the market's next upward move. Spurred by the Baby Boomers' pouring money into the market. To provide for their own retirement. But the

NAME _____ DATE _____ SCORE _____

lessons learned from the Crash of '29 and the cyclical nature of the market have to be relearned by each succeeding generation. Will the current mania and rampant speculation lead to tomorrow's Black Tuesday? Or Black Wednesday? When the retiring Boomers are forced to withdraw their funds from the stock market to finance their lifestyles.

NAME _____ DATE _____ SCORE _____

EXERCISE 24: Revising Sentence Fragments

Identify the sentence fragments in the following passage and correct each one by attaching the absolute phrase to the clause it modifies or by substituting a verb for the participle or infinitive in the absolute phrase. Write your changes between the lines.

    The domestic responsibilities of colonial women were many. Their fates sealed by the absence of the mechanical devices that have eased the burdens of women in recent years. Washing clothes, for instance, was a complicated procedure. The primary problem being the moving of some 50 gallons of water from a pump or well to the stove (for heating) and washtub (for soaking and scrubbing). Home cooking also presented difficulties. The main challenges for the housewife being the danger of inadvertently poisoning her family and the rarity of ovens. Even much later, housework was extremely time-consuming,

NAME _____ DATE _____ SCORE _____

especially for rural and low-income families. Their access to labor-saving devices remaining relatively limited. (Just before World War II, for instance, only 35 percent of farm residences in the United States had electricity.) (Adapted from Susan Strasser, *Never Done: A History of American Housework*)

NAME _____ DATE _____ SCORE _____

EXERCISE 25: Revising Sentence Fragments

Identify the fragments in this paragraph and correct them by attaching each fragment to the independent clause containing the word or word group the appositive modifies. Write your changes between the lines.

    Malls dominate the shopping and the popular cultural center of many cities, offering a myriad of stores and entertainment for people of all ages. Most malls are centered around an anchor store, an outlet of a large national chain. Such as Sears or Penney's or Marshalls. In addition, many smaller, specialty stores are housed in the mall. For example, Nordic Trak, Walden Books, kitchen shops, and computer stores. These stores feature a variety of merchandise targeted to specific hobbies or interests. The exercise enthusiast, the voracious reader, the gourmand, and the technophile. After hours of shopping, customers are ready to eat. Malls anticipate this need by providing a plethora of food establishments from food courts to sit-down restaurants. Hamburgers, to pizzas, to Chinese food, to buffets, to haute cuisine. Entertainment is offered too. Carousel rides for children to video arcades for teenagers to the multi-screened theaters for all ages. Other than shopping, eating, and playing, many people find the malls convenient gathering places to meet friends, to exercise, or just to escape inclement weather. For example, large groups of teens in the main concourse. Older people walking laps around the concourse. The mall has become almost like a home away from home for many people.

NAME _____ DATE _____ SCORE _____

EXERCISE 26: Revising Sentence Fragments

Identify the sentence fragments in this passage and correct them by attaching each detached compound to the rest of the sentence. Write your changes between the lines.

One of the phenomena of the 1990s is the number of parents determined to raise "super-babies." Many affluent parents, professionals themselves, seem driven to raise children who are mentally superior. And physically fit as well. To this end, they enroll babies as young as a few weeks old in baby gyms. And sign up slightly older preschool children for classes that teach computer skills or violin. Or swimming or Japanese. Such classes are important. But are not the only source of formal education for very young children. Parents themselves try to raise their babies' IQs. Or learn to teach toddlers to read or to do simple math. Some parents begin teaching

NAME _____ DATE _____ SCORE _____

with flash cards when their babies are only a few months—or days—old. Others wait until their children are a bit older. And enroll them in day-care programs designed to sharpen their skills. Or spend thousands of dollars on "educational toys." Some psychologists and child-care professionals are favorably impressed by this trend toward earlier and earlier education. But most have serious reservations, feeling the emphasis on academics and pressure to achieve may stunt children's social and emotional growth.

NAME _____ DATE _____ SCORE _____

EXERCISE 27: Revising Sentence Fragments

Identify the fragments in the following paragraph and correct each one by adding, deleting, or changing words to create a complete independent clause. Write your changes between the lines.

    The pursuit of the aquatic species. Otherwise known as the sport of fishing, encompasses a variety of choices depending on one's locale. Coastal residents are afforded the opportunity to fish for a multitude of salt-water species. Including shallow water dwellers such as bone fish, snook, and tarpon. Deep water inhabitants such as red snapper, amberjack, and tuna. Although inland fishermen may not have the number of species to choose from. They have a much larger variety of watery locales such as rivers, lakes, creeks, and ponds. Harboring the common species of bass, bream, and catfish among others. Techniques and tackle used depend on

NAME _____ DATE _____ SCORE _____

the locale. From the large spooled and heavy-lined salt-water reel to the bait-casting reel to the cane pole. These reels can be installed on a large range of rods and line combinations. From bamboo to fiberglass to exotic composites of space-age materials. In addition, the fisherman is faced with the choice of several types of bait. Artificial lures to live bait fish to the lowly worm. Regardless of where one chooses to fish or what type of rig is used. Fishing provides two benefits. Fare for the table and a great source of relaxation and pleasure. As an old sage once said, "Since the earth is two-thirds water. Man should spend two-thirds of his time fishing."

NAME _____ DATE _____ SCORE _____

EXERCISE 28: Revising Comma Splices and Fused Sentences

Find the comma splices and fused sentences in the following paragraph. Correct each in one of the four possible ways listed on pages 79–81 in *The* Brief *Holt Handbook*. If a sentence is correct, leave it alone. Write your corrections between the lines.

EXAMPLE: The fans rose in their seats, the game was over.

The fans rose in their seats; the game was over.

The fans rose in their seats, for the game was over.

Writing with a word processor has made editing papers much easier, many corrections can be made with a simple keystroke. No longer is it necessary to correct non-standard punctuation by hand running the risk of introducing new errors during the editing stage is now virtually eliminated. The essay that has been saved on disk or in hard memory can simply be restored to the

NAME _____ DATE _____ SCORE _____

screen for viewing the corrections can then be inserted into the text and re-saved. The ease of this process has made writers more likely to proofread their work with care, this results in a better quality of work as well as improved grades. Although the computer does not preclude the need for learning the rules that govern standard editing, it has made applying those rules more simple and less time consuming. For most students the days of laboriously handwriting or typing multiple drafts of essays are gone, the computer has closed that chapter of the writing process.

NAME _____ DATE _____ SCORE _____

EXERCISE 29: Sentence Combining

Combine each of the following sentence pairs into one sentence without creating comma splices or fused sentences. In each case, either connect the clauses into a compound sentence with a semicolon or with a comma and a coordinating conjunction, or subordinate one clause to the other to create a complex sentence. You may have to add, delete, reorder, or change words or punctuation.

1. Several recent studies indicate that many American high school students have a poor sense of history. This is affecting our future as a democratic nation and as individuals.

2. Surveys show that nearly one-third of American seventeen-year-olds cannot identify the countries the United States fought against in World War II. One-third think Columbus reached the New World after 1750.

NAME _____ DATE _____ SCORE _____

3. Several reasons have been given for this decline in historical literacy. The main reason is the way history is taught.

4. This problem is bad news. The good news is that there is increasing agreement among educators about what is wrong with current methods of teaching history.

5. History can be exciting and engaging. Too often it is presented in a boring manner.

6. Students are typically expected to memorize dates, facts, and figures. History as adventure—as a "good story"—is frequently neglected.

NAME _____ DATE _____ SCORE _____

7. One way to avoid this problem is to use good textbooks. Texts should be accurate, lively, and focused.

8. Another way to create student interest in historical events is to use primary sources instead of so-called comprehensive textbooks. Autobiographies, journals, and diaries can give students insight into larger issues.

9. Students can also be challenged to think about history by taking sides in a debate. They can learn more about connections among historical events by writing essays rather than taking multiple-choice tests.

10. Finally, history teachers should be less concerned about specific historical details. They should be more concerned about conveying the wonder of history.

NAME _____ DATE _____ SCORE _____

EXERCISE 30: Subject-Verb Agreement

Each of these ten sentences is correct. Read the sentences carefully and explain why each verb form is used in each case.

EXAMPLE: *Harold and Maude* is a popular cult film.

(The verb is singular because the subject *Harold and Maude* is the title of an individual work, even though it is plural in form.)

1. Jack Kerouac, along with Allen Ginsberg and William S. Burroughs, was a major figure in the "beat" movement.

2. Every American boy and girl needs to learn basic computational skills.

3. Aesthetics is not an exact science.

4. The audience was restless.

NAME _____ DATE _____ SCORE _____

5. The Beatles' *Sergeant Pepper* album is one of those albums that remain popular long after the time they are issued.

6. All is quiet.

7. The subject was roses.

8. When he was young, Benjamin Franklin's primary concern was books.

9. Fifty dollars is too much to spend on one concert ticket.

10. "There are more things in heaven and earth, Horatio, than are dreamt of in your philosophy."

EXERCISE 31: Subject-Verb Agreement

Some of these sentences are correct, but others illustrate common errors in subject-verb agreement. If a sentence is correct, mark it with a *C*; if it has an error, correct it.

1. Brad finds that repetitive work violates his low boredom threshold.

2. Peggy, however, is capable of focusing on menial tasks for hours on end.

3. Both the subject and the verb has to agree in number for the sentence to be correct.

4. If otters, fish, and insects swims in the same pond, some will be eaten by the others.

5. Neither country music nor rap appeal to me.

NAME _____ DATE _____ SCORE _____

6. The tree filled with birdhouses attract many different species of birds.

7. Twenty dollars is the average cost of a tank of gasoline.

8. No matter how many people enter the contest, only one of the contestants are going to win the prize.

9. Either the dog or the kittens have to stay outside.

10. Successfully completing a task is always satisfying.

Copyright © 1998 by Harcourt Brace & Company. All rights reserved.

NAME _____ DATE _____ SCORE _____

EXERCISE 32: Subject-Verb, Pronoun-Antecedent Agreement

Find and correct any errors in subject-verb and/or pronoun-antecedent agreement. Write your changes between the lines.

1. Recorded music is available on records, tapes, and compact discs which can be bought at a variety of stores.

2. Vinyl records has been replaced in popularity by the compact disc.

3. Although some bargains are available, a collector can invest a large sum on their music library.

4. The quality of sound reproduction was greatly enhanced with the change from records to compact discs.

5. Unlike records and tapes which can lose its sound quality because of needle scratches, discs may lasts forever.

6. Compact discs use a new digital technology which were unavailable when records were popular.

NAME _____ DATE _____ SCORE _____

7. Every audiophile delight in showing off their music collection and equipment.

8. Considering the range of music available, discs make an ideal gift for birthday and Christmas.

9. In spite of its advantages, the one drawback to compact discs is the inability to record music.

10. The nostalgia many feel for the vinyl records will someday be felt for discs when it is replaced by the silicon chip.

NAME _____ DATE _____ SCORE _____

EXERCISE 33: Subject-Verb, Pronoun-Antecedent Agreement

The following ten sentences illustrate correct subject-verb and pronoun-antecedent agreement. After following the instructions in parentheses after each sentence, revise each so its verbs and pronouns agree with the newly created subject.

EXAMPLE: One child in ten suffers from a learning disability. (Change *One child in ten* to *Ten percent of all children.*)

Ten percent of all children suffer from a learning disability.

1. The governess is seemingly pursued by evil as she tries to protect Miles and Flora from those she feels seek to possess the children's souls. (Change *The governess* to *The governess and the cook.*)

2. Insulin-dependent diabetics are now able to take advantage of new technology that can help alleviate their symptoms. (Change *diabetics* to *The diabetic.*)

NAME _____ DATE _____ SCORE _____

3. All homeowners in shore regions worry about the possible effects of a hurricane on their property. (Change *All homeowners* to *Every homeowner.*)

4. Federally funded job-training programs offer unskilled workers an opportunity to acquire skills they can use to secure employment. (Change *workers* to *the worker.*)

5. Foreign imports pose a major challenge to the American automobile market. (Change *Foreign imports* to *The foreign import.*)

6. *Brideshead Revisited* tells how one family and its devotion to its Catholic faith affect Charles Ryder. (Delete *and its devotion to its Catholic faith.*)

NAME _____ DATE _____ SCORE _____

7. *Writer's Digest* and *The Writer* are designed to aid writers as they seek markets for their work. (Change *writers* to *the writer*.)

8. Most American families have access to television; in fact, more have televisions than have indoor plumbing. (Change *Most American families* to *Almost every American family*.)

9. In Montana it seems as though every town's elevation is higher than its population. (Change *every town's elevation* to *All the towns' elevations*.)

10. A woman without a man is like a fish without a bicycle. (Change *A woman/a man* to *Women/men*.)

NAME _____ DATE _____ SCORE _____

EXERCISE 34: Principal Parts

Complete the sentences in the following paragraph with an appropriate form of the verbs in parentheses.

EXAMPLE: Many writers have _____ stories of intrigue and suspense. (weave)

Many writers have _woven_ stories of intrigue and suspense.

Eric Blair, a well-known British novelist and essayist, _____ (choose) to use the pseudonym George Orwell. His essay "A Hanging," _____ (take) from his book *Shooting an Elephant and Other Essays,* is _____ (write) in narrative form. It describes a morning in Burma when Orwell observed the execution of a prisoner who was to be _____ (hang) for his crime. One of the most startling scenes in the essay comes at the end when the onlookers, _____ (forsake) the seriousness of the moment, leave the prison yard after the event, laughing on their way to have a drink.

NAME _____ DATE _____ SCORE _____

EXERCISE 35: Principal Parts

Complete the following sentences with the appropriate form of the appropriate verb in parentheses.

    EXAMPLE: John McKeever _____ down the gauntlet. (laid, lay)

        John McKeever __lay__ down the gauntlet.

1. Distracted by all the noise, Ray did not notice that he had _____ on a freshly painted bench. (sat, set)

2. Having practiced all morning, the band played as _____ as they had ever performed. (well, good)

3. The condemned man was sentenced to be _____ in the town square at sunrise. (hanged, hung)

4. _____ in the hot sun all day can result in a severe sunburn. (Laying, Lying).

5. Even though his engine was not running _____, the stock car driver ran a _____ race. (good, well)

NAME _____ DATE _____ SCORE _____

EXERCISE 36: Tense

A verb is missing from each of the following sentences. Fill in the form of the verb indicated in parentheses after each sentence.

EXAMPLE: Gambling, although illegal for years in America, _____ (be: present) now allowed in many states.

Gambling, although illegal for years in America, is now allowed in many states.

1. The colonists who _____ (settle: past) the country, often _____ (engage: past) in various types of wagering.

2. Accounts of gaming _____ (be: present perfect) included in many history books.

3. Eventually, the Puritans enforced their social mores, _____ (result: present participle) in many forms of gambling being made illegal.

NAME _____ DATE _____ SCORE _____

4. Horse racing and bingo, however, _____ (continue: past perfect) to be accepted by society.

5. The fiercely independent inhabitants of Nevada _____ (break: past) the taboo by using state law to legalize gambling in Las Vegas.

6. Using obscure federal laws, Native Americans _____ (operate: present perfect progressive) their own gaming establishments for years.

7. Now other states, realizing an ever increasing need for sources of revenue, _____ (follow: present progressive) Navada's lead.

8. To comply with the off-shore gambling laws, states _____ (begin: past perfect) to build casinos on riverboats.

NAME _____ DATE _____ SCORE _____

9. States not having inland waterways now _____ (zone: present) special locations for landlocked casinos.

10. If society can overcome the adverse effects of gaming, gamblers _____ (enjoy: future progressive) this pleasurable entertainment in many more places.

NAME _____ DATE _____ SCORE _____

EXERCISE 37: Tense

From inside each pair of parentheses, choose the correct verb form. Make certain you use the correct sequence of tenses.

> **EXAMPLE:** Sophocles _____ (won, had won) his first victory in the Athenian spring drama competition in 468 B.C.
>
> Sophocles ____won____ his first victory in the Athenian spring drama competition in 468 B.C.

1. In Sophocles' famous tragedy *Oedipus Rex*, Oedipus _____ (declares, declared) that the murderer of King Laios, his predecessor to the throne, will be found and removed from the city of Thebes.

2. His declaration comes after he _____ (learned, has learned) that the presence of the murderer has caused the plague on the city.

NAME _____ DATE _____ SCORE _____

3. Sophocles _____ (was, is) one of the three great ancient Creek writers of tragedy; in keeping with the characteristics of tragedy, he portrayed Oedipus as a character with a tragic flaw.

4. By the time Oedipus learns of the presence of the murderer in the city, the citizens _____ (gave, have given) up hope of restoring the city to its former glory.

5. Oedipus came to the city just after King Laios' death, and when he solved the riddle of the Sphinx, he _____ (becomes, became) the new king.

6. Having been widowed as a result of the king's death, Queen Iocaste _____ (had married, married) Oedipus.

NAME _____ DATE _____ SCORE _____

7. When the blind prophet Tiresias says that Oedipus is the murderer being sought, Oedipus _____ (accused, accuses) Tiresias of being involved in a plot against him.

8. In spite of his protestations, Oedipus _____ (learned, learns) that he is indeed the murderer and, worse, the son of his wife.

NAME _____ DATE _____ SCORE _____

EXERCISE 38: Mood

Complete the sentences in the following paragraph by inserting the appropriate form (indicative, imperative, or subjunctive) of the verb in parentheses.

Harry Houdini was a famous escape artist. He _____ (perform) escapes from every type of bond imaginable: handcuffs, locks, straitjackets, ropes, sacks, and sealed chests underwater. In Germany workers _____ (challenge) Houdini to escape from a packing box. If he _____ (be) to escape, they would admit that he _____ (be) the best escape artist in the world. Houdini accepted. Before getting into the box he asked that the observers _____ (give) it a thorough examination. He then asked that a worker _____ (nail) him in the box. "_____ (place) a screen around the box," he ordered after he had been sealed inside. In a few minutes Houdini _____ (step) from behind the screen. When the workers demanded that they _____ (see) the box, Houdini pulled down the screen. To their surprise they saw the box with the lid still nailed tightly in place.

EXERCISE 39: Voice

In each of the following sentences, underline the subject once and the predicate twice. Then indicate in the blanks which verbs are active and which are passive. Comment below on why active voice and passive voice are used as they are in these sentences.

_____ 1. The stock market as we know it today began when merchants met under a tree at the intersection of Broad and Wall Streets in New York City.

_____ 2. This popular landmark was accepted by local merchants as a convenient meeting place to buy, sell, and trade their wares.

_____ 3. Gradually as the number of traders increased, written contracts were required as a form of binding legal agreement for their transactions.

_____ 4. These contracts represented ownership of shares of individual companies; subsequently, traders referred to these shares as stock certificates.

NAME _____ DATE _____ SCORE _____

_____ 5. To avoid inclement weather, the traders moved into a building which houses the present location of the New York Stock Exchange on Wall Street.

_____ 6. The advent of electronic communications allowed widespread trading of stock throughout the country.

NAME _____ DATE _____ SCORE _____

EXERCISE 40: Voice

Determine which verbs in the following paragraph should be changed from the passive to the active voice. Between the lines rewrite the sentences containing these verbs. Explain your changes below.

    Rockets were invented by the Chinese about A.D. 1000. Gunpowder was packed into bamboo tubes and ignited by means of a fuse. These rockets were fired by soldiers at enemy armies and usually caused panic. In thirteenth-century England an improved form of gunpowder was introduced by Roger Bacon. As a result, rockets were used in battles and were a common—although unreliable—weapon. In the early eighteenth century a twenty-pound rocket that traveled almost two miles was constructed by William Congreve, an English artillery expert. By the late nineteenth century thought was given to supersonic speeds by the physicist Ernst Mach.

NAME _____ DATE _____ SCORE _____

The sonic boom was predicted by him. The first liquid-fuel rocket was launched by the American Robert Goddard in 1926. A pamphlet written by him anticipated almost all future rocket developments. As a result of his pioneering work, he is called the father of modern rocketry.

NAME _____ DATE _____ SCORE _____

EXERCISE 41: Voice

Determine which sentences in the following paragraph would be more effective in the passive voice. Rewrite those sentences between the lines. Explain the reasons for your choices below.

The Regent Diamond is one of the world's most famous and coveted jewels. A slave discovered the 410-carat diamond in 1701 in an Indian mine. Over the years, people stole and sold the diamond several times. In 1717, the Regent of France bought the diamond for an enormous sum, but during the French Revolution, it disappeared again. Someone later found it in a ditch in Paris. Eventually, Napoleon had the diamond set into his ceremonial sword. At last, when the French monarch fell, the government placed the Regent Diamond in the Louvre, where it still remains to be enjoyed by all.

NAME _____ DATE _____ SCORE _____

EXERCISE 42: Pronoun Case

Underline the correct form of the pronoun within the parentheses. Be prepared to explain why you chose each form.

EXAMPLE: Tony, Ninfa, and (they, them) wanted to go to the Living Museum which featured dinosaurs.

1. Robert E. Lee and (he, him) commanded opposing armies during the War Between the States.

2. Jayme called (he, him) to make sure George was home before driving all the way to Panama City.

3. Both (she, her) and Carl Sagan, the renowned, award-winning astronomer, collaborated on the PBS broadcast of *Cosmos*.

4. Joey said to John, "To avoid hurting anyone's feelings, let's keep the information between you and (I, me)."

NAME _____ DATE _____ SCORE _____

5. The Critical Thinking class made clear to (us, we) the difference between believing and knowing.

6. Philip, (who, whom) punched the wrong button on his cellular phone, called Brad rather than Cheryl.

7. (We, Us) store owners often get false burglar alarms which are annoying and time consuming.

8. I understand (you, your) being disappointed that the game was delayed because of the unexpected storm.

9. The salesperson asked Len and (me, I) to complete our purchases as the store was about to close.

NAME _____ DATE _____ SCORE _____

EXERCISE 43: Sentence Combining

Using the word in the parentheses, combine each pair of sentences into a single sentence. You may change word order or add or delete words.

EXAMPLE: Stephen King is one of the best-selling popular authors of the twentieth century. He writes primarily horror novels. (who)

Stephen King, who writes primarily horror novels, is one of the best-selling popular authors of the twentieth century.

1. Toni Morrison is an award-winning American writer. Her subject matter most often focuses on African-American themes. (who)

2. Robin Cook, another popular writer, holds a medical degree. His subjects exclusively deal with common people caught up in exotic medical dilemmas. (who)

NAME _____ DATE _____ SCORE _____

3. Steve Nison wrote *Japanese Candlestick Charting Techniques* in 1990. He also wrote a companion book, *Beyond Candlesticks*, in 1994. (who)

4. Erle Stanley Gardner wrote numerous detective mysteries. His most famous character was Perry Mason, the well-known attorney who lost only one case in his entire career. (who)

5. Ayn Rand is the icon of generations of college-aged students. Two of her works, *Atlas Shrugged* and *The Fountainhead*, remain perennial best sellers. (who)

NAME _____ DATE _____ SCORE _____

EXERCISE 44: Pronoun Reference

Write the name of the pronoun error in the blank to the left of the following sentences. Then revise each sentence by substituting an appropriate noun or noun phrase for the underlined pronoun.

EXAMPLE: The supervisor asked Margaret to chair the evaluation team, and Margaret selected <u>him</u> as her associate.

ANALYSIS: <u>Him</u> refers to a nonexistent antecedent.

REVISION: The supervisor asked Margaret to chair the evaluation team, and Margaret selected Danny as her associate.

_____ 1. The purpose of the evaluation was to determine the quality of each employee's work. The customers' complaints increased the need for <u>it</u>.

_____ 2. The review of fifteen employees was so time consuming that <u>they</u> were unable to complete it alone.

_____ 3. The committee devised an evaluation form which could be used as a guideline. <u>It</u> made the process much easier.

NAME _____ DATE _____ SCORE _____

_____ 4. Having seen the form, the supervisor was convinced (he, she, they) would be successful with the assigned project.

_____ 5. Once the evaluation was completed, complaints were greatly reduced. <u>This</u> was precisely the results the supervisor wanted.

_____ 6. In celebration of <u>their</u> success, Margaret decided to treat the staff and customers to a party.

_____ 7. At the party <u>they</u> all agreed that the evaluations were the best thing the company had ever done.

_____ 8. After having agreed that the company was on the right track, <u>she</u> decided to expand the evaluations to other problem areas.

_____ 9. Margaret talked with another woman who suggested that an employee "suggestion box" would be a good way to determine where improvements might be made; <u>she</u> decided to implement this idea as quickly as possible.

NAME _____ DATE _____ SCORE _____

_____ 10. On the next workday, the suggestion box was placed near the front desk. The staff found <u>it</u> a useful way of making their complaints known.

NAME _____ DATE _____ SCORE _____

EXERCISE 45: Modification

Revise each of the incorrect sentences in this paragraph so that only adjectives modify nouns and pronouns and only adverbs modify verbs, adjectives, or other adverbs. Be sure to eliminate informal forms. Write your corrections between the lines below.

The most popular self-help trend in the United States today is subliminal tapes. These tapes, with titles like "How to Attract Love," "Freedom from Acne, and "I Am a Genius," are intended to solve every problem known to modern society—quick and easy. The tapes are said to work because their "hidden messages" bypass conscious defense mechanisms. The listener hears only music or relaxing sounds, like waves rolling slow and steady. At decibel levels perceived only subconsciously, positive words and phrases are embedded, usually by someone who speaks deep and rhythmic. The top-selling cassettes are those

NAME _____ DATE _____ SCORE _____

to help you lose weight or quit smoking. The popularity of such tapes is not hard to understand. They promise easy solutions to complex problems. But the main benefit of these tapes appears to be for the sellers, who are accumulating profits real fast.

NAME _____ DATE _____ SCORE _____

EXERCISE 46: Sentence Modeling

Being careful to use adjectives—not adverbs—as subject complements and object complements, write five sentences in imitation of each of the following. Be sure to use five different linking verbs in your imitations of each sentence.

1. Julie looked worried.

2. Dan considers his collection valuable.

NAME _____ DATE _____ SCORE _____

EXERCISE 47: Comparative and Superlative Forms

Supply the correct comparative and superlative forms for each of the following adjectives or adverbs. Then use each form in a sentence.

EXAMPLE: strange   stranger   strangest

The story had a strange ending. The explanation sounded stranger each time I heard it. This is the strangest gadget I have ever seen.

1. many

2. eccentric

3. confusing

Copyright © 1998 by Harcourt Brace & Company. All rights reserved.

NAME _____ DATE _____ SCORE _____

4. bad

5. mysterious

6. softly

7. embarrassing

8. well

NAME _____ DATE _____ SCORE _____

9. often

10. tiny

11. easy

12. judicious

NAME _____ DATE _____ SCORE _____

EXERCISE 48: Nouns as Modifiers

Underline every noun used as a modifier in the following passage. Then revise where necessary to eliminate clumsy or unclear phrasing created by overuse of nouns as modifiers. Try substituting adjective or possessive forms and rearrange word order where you feel it is indicated. Write your changes between the lines.

    The student government business management trainee program is extremely popular on campus. The student government donated some of the seed money to begin this management trainee program, which is one of the most successful the university business school has ever offered to undergraduate students. Three core courses must be taken before the student intern can actually begin work. First, a management theory course is given every spring semester in conjunction with the business school. Then, the following fall semester, students in the trainee program are required to

NAME _____ DATE _____ SCORE _____

take a course in personnel practices, including employee benefits. Finally, they take a business elective.

During the summer, the student interns are placed in junior management positions in large electronics, manufacturing, or public utility companies. This job experience is considered the most valuable part of the program because it gives students a taste of the work world.

NAME _____ DATE _____ SCORE _____

EXERCISE 49: Combining for Variety

Using coordination, subordination, and embedding, revise this string of choppy simple sentences into a more varied and interesting paragraph. Write your changes between the lines below.

The Authorized Version of the Bible was first published in 1611. The Authorized Version of the Bible is often referred to as the King James Version. It involved several years of work by numerous scholars. Much of the year prior to its publication was devoted to final preparations. After it had been prepared, the document was sent to press. Many steps were taken during those final months. One step involved calling upon writers of the day. Several of the writers were eminent. They were needed to "refine" this translation. It was the most recent English translation. These writers devoted their efforts to the

NAME _____ DATE _____ SCORE _____

project. They enhanced the poetic qualities of Proverbs. They enhanced the poetic qualities of the Song of Solomon. And they enhanced the poetic qualities of the Psalms.

NAME _____ DATE _____ SCORE _____

EXERCISE 50: Combining for Variety

A. Combine each of the following sentence groups into one long sentence.

B. Then, compose a relatively short sentence to follow each long one.

C. Finally, combine all the sentences into a paragraph, adding any transitions necessary for coherence. Proofread your paragraph to be sure that the sentences are varied in length.

1. The King James Version of the Bible is the subject of many literary legends. One of the legends is intriguing. It alleges that Shakespeare's hand is present in the King James Version of the Bible. More specifically, though, it alleges that Shakespeare's hand is present in the 46th Psalm.

NAME _____ DATE _____ SCORE _____

2. Count to the forty-sixth word from the beginning of the psalm. You will find that it is *shake*. Then identify the forty-sixth word form the end of the psalm. You will find that it is *spear*.

3. The situation becomes even more intriguing. It becomes even more intriguing when we realize that when the revision work was underway in 1610. It becomes even more intriguing when we also realize that Shakespeare was forty-six years old in 1610.

EXERCISE 51: Revising for Variety

Revise the compound sentences in this passage so the sentence structure is varied and the writer's meaning and emphasis are clear. Write your changes between the lines.

Leonardo da Vinci's *The Last Supper* is one of the most easily recognized works of art. It was produced during Leonardo's residence in Milan. Leonardo was under the patronage of Duke Sforza. Leonardo used oil and tempera for *The Last Supper*. He used a wall in the refectory of Santa Maria della Grazie as his "canvas." Even the most casual art observer has viewed a copy of *The Last Supper*. But few serious students of art realize that it is actually a mural. It measures 14'–5" × 28'. It is surprising Leonardo completed his work on such a large scale. It is surprising to many who have seen only small replicas. Many of these replicas are the size of a post card.

NAME _____ DATE _____ SCORE _____

Giorgio Vasari records an interesting anecdote. Giorgio Vasari was an Italian art historian. He lived during the sixteenth century. The anecdote concerns Leonardo's use of models. These models were used for *The Last Supper*. Leonardo drew the disciples from life. Leonardo encountered difficulty in locating a suitable Judas Iscariot. While he worked on the painting, Leonardo met with some problems. Leonardo was troubled by the prior of Santa Maria. The prior monitored the work's progress. He monitored from a vantage uncomfortably close for Leonardo. The prior expressed his concerns to Duke Sforza. Leonardo heard that the prior had complained to the duke. Leonardo mentioned that any delay he had experienced was merely the result of his having encountered difficulty in

NAME _____ DATE _____ SCORE _____

identifying a model. The model was for the betrayer. Leonardo pointed out that he would be delayed no longer. He had located his model. The prior would serve nicely.

NAME _____ DATE _____ SCORE _____

EXERCISE 52: Revising for Variety

The following paragraph is composed entirely of declarative sentences. To make it more varied, add three sentences—one exclamation, one rhetorical question, and one command—anywhere in the paragraph. Be sure the sentences you create are consistent with the paragraph's purpose and tone. Write your changes between the lines.

When the Fourth of July comes around, the nation explodes with patriotism. Everywhere we look we see parades and picnics, firecrackers, and fireworks. An outsider might wonder what all the fuss is about. We could explain that this is America's birthday party, and all the candles are being lit at once. There is no reason for us to hold back our enthusiasm—or to limit the noise that celebrates it. The Fourth of July is watermelon and corn on the cob, American flags and sparklers, brass bands, and more. Everyone looks forward to this celebration, and everyone has a good time.

NAME _____ DATE _____ SCORE _____

EXERCISE 53: Opening Strategies

Each of these sentences begins with the subject. Rewrite each so that it has a different opening and then identify the opening strategy you used.

EXAMPLE: N. Scott Momaday, the prominent Native American writer, tells the story of his first fourteen years in *The Names*.

REVISED: Prominent Native American writer N. Scott Momaday tells the story of his first fourteen years in *The Names*. (appositive)

1. Momaday was taken as a very young child to Devil's Tower, the geological formation in Wyoming that is called Tsoai (Bear Tree) in Kiowa, and there he was given the name Tsoai-talee (Bear Tree Boy).

NAME _____ DATE _____ SCORE _____

2. The Kiowa myth of the origin of Tsoai is about a boy who playfully chases his seven sisters up a tree, which rises into the air as the boy is transformed into a bear.

3. The boy-bear becomes increasingly ferocious and claws the bark of the tree, which becomes a great rock with a flat top and deeply scored sides.

NAME _____ DATE _____ SCORE _____

4. The sisters climb higher and higher to escape their brother's wrath, and eventually they become the seven stars of the Big Dipper.

5. This story, from which Momaday received one of his names, appears as a constant in his works—*The Way to Rainy Mountain, House Made of Dawn,* and *The Ancient Child.*

NAME _____ DATE _____ SCORE _____

EXERCISE 54: Revising for Variety

The following sentences use conventional word order. Revise each in one of two ways:

1. Invert the sentence.

   OR

2. Vary the word order by placing words between subject and verb.

EXAMPLE: Exam week is invariably hectic and not much fun.

Invariably hectic and not much fun is exam week.
or

Exam week, invariably hectic, is not much fun.

1. The Beach Boys formed a band in 1961, and the group consisted of Brian Wilson, his brothers Carl and Dennis, their cousin Mike Love, and Alan Jardine, a friend.

NAME _____ DATE _____ SCORE _____

2. The group's first single was "Surfin'," which attracted national attention.

3. Capitol Records signed the band to record "Surfin' Safari" because the company felt the group had potential.

4. The Beach Boys had many other top-twenty singles during the next five years, and most of these hits were written, arranged, and produced by Brian Wilson.

NAME _____ DATE _____ SCORE _____

5. Their songs focused on California sun and good times and included "I Get Around," "Be True to Your School," "Fun, Fun, Fun," and "Good Vibrations."

NAME _____ DATE _____ SCORE _____

EXERCISE 55: Revising for Emphasis

Revise the following sentences to make them more emphatic. For each, decide which ideas should be highlighted and group key phrases at sentence beginnings or endings, using climactic order or inverted order where appropriate.

1. Police want to upgrade their firepower because criminals are better armed than ever before.

2. A few years ago felons used so-called Saturday night specials, small-caliber six-shot revolvers.

NAME _____ DATE _____ SCORE _____

3. Now semiautomatic pistols capable of firing fifteen to twenty rounds, along with paramilitary weapons like the AK-47, have replaced these weapons.

4. Police are adopting such weapons as new fast-firing shotguns and 9mm automatic pistols in order to gain an equal footing with their adversaries.

5. Faster reloading and a hair trigger are among the numerous advantages that automatic pistols, the weapons of choice among law enforcement officers, have over the traditional .38-caliber police revolver.

NAME _____ DATE _____ SCORE _____

EXERCISE 56: Revising for Emphasis

Revise the sentences in these paragraphs, using parallelism and balance whenever possible to highlight corresponding elements and using repetition of key words and phrases to add emphasis. (To achieve repetition, you must change some synonyms.) You may combine sentences, and you may add, delete, or reorder words. Write your changes between the lines.

For hundreds and thousands of years, the Nile Valley experienced an annual flood. The yearly floodwaters of the Nile carried soil particles from upstream. The soil particles were deposited throughout the flood plain. The silt deposited by the yearly flood renewed the fertility of the Egyptian fields. This yearly event might be interpreted as a natural disaster. Rather than being a natural disaster, the annual flood permitted the rise of one of the richest of ancient civilizations. It was also one of the most advanced ancient civilizations. The annual flood enabled the people to grow enough food to support a large population. There was enough food for people for other activities. Some of these activities include building, scholarship, and art.

During the past century, the Aswan High Dam was constructed. There have been enormous changes in the Nile Valley. The Aswan High Dam is designed to retain an entire annual flow of the Nile. The Aswan High Dam also provides power to make cheap fertilizers. These fertilizers are needed by the intensively cultivated farms that are no longer covered by silty Nile water, which had previously renewed soil fertility. The Aswan High Dam has ended the annual flooding of the Nile Valley. The Nile used to bring nutritious silt to the region. The nutritious silt was once cherished for its nutrients.

NAME _____ DATE _____ SCORE _____

Many people now consider the silt a nuisance. The silt is considered a nuisance because it fills up irrigation canals.

NAME _____ DATE _____ SCORE _____

EXERCISE 57: Active Voice for Emphasis

Revise this paragraph to eliminate awkward or excessive use of passive constructions. Write your changes between the lines.

    Jack Dempsey, the heavyweight champion between 1919 and 1926, had an interesting but uneven career. He was considered one of the greatest boxers of all time. Dempsey began fighting as "Kid Blackie," but his career didn't take off until 1919, when Jack "Doc" Kearns became his manager. Dempsey won the championship when Jess Willard was defeated by him in Toledo, Ohio, in 1919. Dempsey immediately became a popular sports figure; Franklin Delano Roosevelt was one of his biggest fans. Influential friends were made by Jack Dempsey. Boxing lessons were given by him to the actor Rudolph Valentino. He made friends with Douglas

NAME _____ DATE _____ SCORE _____

Fairbanks, Sr., Damon Runyon, and J. Paul Getty. Hollywood serials were made by Dempsey, but the title was lost by him to Gene Tunney, and Dempsey failed to regain it the following year. Meanwhile, his life was marred by unpleasant developments such as a bitter legal battle with his manager and his 1920 indictment for draft evasion. In subsequent years, after his boxing career declined, a restaurant was opened by Dempsey, and many major sporting events were attended by him. This exposure kept him in the public eye until he lost his restaurant. Jack Dempsey died in 1983.

EXERCISE 58: Revising for Conciseness

Revise the following paragraph to eliminate deadwood, utility words, and circumlocution. When a word or phrase seems superfluous, delete it or replace it with a more concise expression. Write your changes between the lines.

Sally Ride is an astrophysicist who was selected to be the first American woman astronaut. It seems that there were many good reasons why she was chosen. She is a first-rate athlete, and she did graduate work in X-ray astronomy and free-electron lasers. As a result of these and other factors, NASA accepted Ride as a "mission specialist" astronaut in the year 1978. Prior to that time, Ride had been a graduate student at Stanford who knew she had the capability of becoming a specialist in the area of theoretical physics. At NASA she helped to design the remote manipulator arm of the space shuttle, and at a later point she relayed flight instructions to

NAME _____ DATE _____ SCORE _____

astronauts until such time as she was assigned to a flight crew. Now, Ride teaches at the University of California. Although she is no longer employed by NASA, at this point in time she remains something quite definitely special: America's very first woman in space.

NAME _____ DATE _____ SCORE _____

EXERCISE 59: Revising for Conciseness

Eliminate any unnecessary repetition of words or ideas in this paragraph. Also revise to eliminate deadwood, utility words, or circumlocution. Write your changes between the lines.

    The seven daughters of Atlas are known as the Pleiades. They were pursued by Orion. Orion was unable to seize any of them. Orion continued to follow them. Orion continued to follow them until Zeus took pity on them. Zeus placed them in the heavens. Seven stars make up the Pleiades. Only six stars are clearly visible. The seventh is invisible except for some people. These people are those who have especially keen vision. In Greek mythology, the seventh star represented Electra. Electra was the mother of Dardanus. Dardanus founded the Trojan race. There is a legend about Electra. The legend held Electra dropped from the sky. Electra did not

NAME _____ DATE _____ SCORE _____

want to look down from the sky. Electra did not want to see the destruction of Troy. Today, though, all seven stars are visible in the Pleiades. Actually, more than seven stars can be seen. But you must use binoculars to see more than seven stars in this cluster. You can even see several hundred stars. But you must use a telescope. Viewing through a telescope will yield several hundred stars.

NAME _____ DATE _____ SCORE _____

EXERCISE 60: Revising for Conciseness

Revise the rambling sentences in this paragraph by eliminating excessive coordination and subordination, unnecessary use of the passive voice, and overuse of wordy prepositional phrases and noun constructions. As you revise, make your sentences more concise by deleting nonessential words and superfluous repetition. Write your changes between the lines.

Orion lost the trail of the Pleiades. Orion became the companion of Artemis. Artemis was a virgin goddess. Artemis was the goddess of the moon. Artemis was also the sister of Apollo. Apollo feared for his sister's chastity. Apollo sent a large scorpion to chase Orion. Orion observed the scorpion enter a body of water. Orion pursued the scorpion. Apollo then persuaded Artemis to shoot the object. The object was bobbing in the waves. Her arrow pierced Orion's head. Artemis was deeply saddened at her loss. Artemis placed Orion's image among the stars. In the stars,

NAME _____ DATE _____ SCORE _____

Orion's image continues to be stalked by the scorpion. The scorpion is also a constellation. Orion and the scorpion are separated. They are separated by a great distance. The Pleiades, however, are in front of Orion. Orion is much closer to the Pleiades. Orion continues to pursue the Pleiades.

NAME _____ DATE _____ SCORE _____

EXERCISE 61: Shifts in Tense, Voice, Mood, Person, Number

Read the following sentences and eliminate any shifts in tense, voice, mood, person, or number. Some sentences are correct, and some will have more than one possible answer. Write your changes between the lines.

1. Gettysburg is a borough of south-central Pennsylvania where some of the bloodiest fighting of the Civil War occurs in July 1863.

2. Giotto was born near Florence in 1267 and is given credit for the revival of painting in the Renaissance.

3. The early Babylonians divided the circle into 360 parts, and the volume of a pyramid could also be calculated by them.

NAME _____ DATE _____ SCORE _____

4. During World War II General Motors expanded its production facilities, and guns, tanks, and ammunition were made.

5. Diamonds, the only gems that are valuable when colorless, were worn to cure disease and to ward off evil spirits.

6. First, clear the area of weeds, and then you should spread the mulch in a six-inch layer.

NAME _____ DATE _____ SCORE _____

7. When one visits the Grand Canyon, you should be sure to notice the fractures and faults on the north side of the Kaibab Plateau.

8. For a wine grape, cool weather means it will have a higher acid content and a sour taste; hot weather means they will have lower acid content and a sweet taste.

9. Mary Wollstonecraft wrote *Vindication of the Rights of Women,* and then she wrote *Vindication of the Rights of Men.*

NAME _____ DATE _____ SCORE _____

10. When you look at the Angora goat, one will see it has an abundant undergrowth.

11. Robert the Bruce defeated the English forces at Bannockburn, and soon thereafter he is recognized as King of Scotland.

12. During the mummification process, the Egyptians placed many of the body's organs in canopic jars; ironically, though, they discarded the brain because they are uncertain of its role.

NAME _____ DATE _____ SCORE _____

13. Scholars have often sought to determine the actual location of Gulliver's Brobdingnag, but you just can't pinpoint it on the map.

14. In spite of a disappointing record of three wins and eleven losses, Coach DeGaetano was proud that the team had maintained a positive attitude and that they received the League Sportsmanship Trophy.

NAME _____ DATE _____ SCORE _____

EXERCISE 62: Shifts from Direct to Indirect Discourse

Transform the direct discourse in the following sentences into indirect discourse. Keep in mind that general truths stay in the present. Write your changes between the lines.

EXAMPLE: Anna Quindlen explained why she kept her maiden name when she married: "It was a political decision, a simple statement that I was somebody and not an adjunct of anybody, especially a husband."

Anna Quindlen explained that she made a decision to keep her maiden name when she married because it expressed a simple political statement that she was somebody and not an adjunct to anybody, especially not to a husband.

1. In cases of possible sexual harassment, Ellen Goodman suggests a "reasonable woman standard" be applied: "How would a reasonable woman interpret this? How would a reasonable woman behave?"

NAME _____ DATE _____ SCORE _____

2. Sally Thane Christensen, advocating the use of an endangered species of tree, the yew, as a treatment for cancer, asked, "Is a tree worth a life?"

3. Stephen Nathanson, considering the morality of the death penalty, asked, "What if the death penalty did save lives?"

4. Martin Luther King, Jr., said, "I have a dream that one day this nation will rise up and live out the true meaning of its creed."

NAME _____ DATE _____ SCORE _____

5. Mohandas K. Gandhi wrote, "Complete civil disobedience is a state of peaceful rebellion—a refusal to obey every single State-made law."

6. Benjamin Franklin once stated, "The older I grow, the more apt I am to doubt my own judgment of others."

7. Speaking of the theater of the absurd in 1962, Edward Albee asked, "Is it, as it has been accused of being, obscure, sordid, destructive, anti-theater, perverse, and absurd (in the sense of foolish)?"

NAME _____ DATE _____ SCORE _____

8. Thoreau said, "The finest qualities of our nature, like the bloom on fruits, can be preserved only by the most delicate handling."

9. In *Death Knocks*, Death asks Nat, "Who should I look like?"

10. In *Death of a Salesman*, Linda stands by her husband's grave after his funeral and asks, "Why didn't anybody come?"

NAME _____ DATE _____ SCORE _____

11. In F. Scott Fitzgerald's *The Great Gatsby*, Jay Gatsby offers this observation about Daisy: "Her voice is full of money."

12. About the importance of fostering family values, Vice President Dan Quayle stated in a 1992 speech, "It's time to talk again about family, hard work, integrity and personal responsibility."

NAME _____ DATE _____ SCORE _____

EXERCISE 63: Mixed Constructions

Revise the following mixed constructions so their parts fit together both grammatically and logically. Write your changes between the lines.

EXAMPLE: By investing in commodities made her rich.

Investing in commodities made her rich.

1. In implementing the "motor voter" bill will make it easier for people to register to vote.

2. She sank the basket was the reason they won the game.

NAME _____ DATE _____ SCORE _____

3. Because of a defect in design was why the roof of the Hartford Stadium collapsed.

4. Since he wants to make his paper clearer is the reason he revises extensively.

5. Even though she works for a tobacco company does not mean that she should be against laws prohibiting smoking in restaurants.

NAME _____ DATE _____ SCORE _____

EXERCISE 64: Faulty Predication

Revise the following sentences to eliminate faulty predication. Keep in mind that each sentence may be revised in more than one way. Write your changes between the lines.

EXAMPLE: The reason there are traffic jams at 9 A.M. and 5 P.M. is because too many people work traditional rather than staggered hours.

REVISED: There are traffic jams at 9 A.M. and 5 P.M. because too many people work traditional rather than staggered hours.

1. Inflation is when the purchasing power of currency declines.

2. Hypertension is where the blood pressure is elevated.

NAME _____ DATE _____ SCORE _____

3. Computers have become part of our everyday lives, such as instant cash machines.

4. Some people say the reason for the increasing violence in American cities is because guns are too easily available.

5. The reason there is congestion in American cities is because there are too many people living too close together.

NAME _____ DATE _____ SCORE _____

EXERCISE 65: Incomplete or Illogical Comparisons

Revise the following sentences to correct any incomplete or illogical comparisons. Write your changes between the lines.

INCOMPLETE: Technology-based industries are concerned about inflation as much as service industries.

COMPLETE: Technology-based industries are concerned about inflation as much as service industries are.

1. Opportunities in technical writing are more promising than business writing.

2. Technical writing is more challenging.

Copyright © 1998 by Harcourt Brace & Company. All rights reserved.

NAME _____ DATE _____ SCORE _____

3. In some ways, technical and business writing require more attention to correctness and are, therefore, more difficult.

4. Business writers are concerned about clarity as much as technical writers.

5. Technology-based industries may one day create more writing opportunities than any industry.

NAME _____ DATE _____ SCORE _____

EXERCISE 66: Using Parallelism

Identify the parallel elements in these sentences by underlining parallel words and bracketing parallel phrases and clauses.

EXAMPLE: Each morning, my roommate amazes me with her energy: she [<u>wakes herself</u> at four o'clock without an alarm], [<u>jogs two miles</u>], [<u>cooks breakfast</u> for both of us], [<u>sends an e-mail</u> to her mother], [<u>calls her boyfriend</u>], and [<u>wears a smile</u> all the while].

1. Angela worked all of her math problems, studied her Spanish assignment, read two history textbook chapters, and then wrote her composition.

2. Long before she began to write professionally, Lindsay had developed a habit of observing people, storing impressions they made upon her, and drawing conclusions about human beings from them.

3. Before making the long journey to Panama City Beach for spring break, take these precautions: change the oil, fill the gas tank, check the tires' air pressure, and replace the windshield wipers.

NAME _____ DATE _____ SCORE _____

4. Brian and Beth agreed that it was one of the best films they'd seen in several months: its characters were believable, its camera work was intriguing, its soundtrack was spectacular, and its language was not offensive.

5. For a fishing trip that's certain to be memorable, my grandfather recommends the following preparations: pack your rod, reel, and tackle box; check the boat's motor; purchase gas and oil; and make plenty of peanut butter and jelly sandwiches.

NAME _____ DATE _____ SCORE _____

EXERCISE 67: Sentence Combining

Combine each of the following sentence pairs or sentence groups into one sentence that uses parallel structure. Be sure all parallel words, phrases, and clauses are expressed in parallel terms.

1. Originally, there were five performing Marx brothers. One was nicknamed Groucho. The others were called Chico, Harpo, Gummo, and Zeppo.

2. Groucho was very well known. So were Chico and Harpo. Gummo soon dropped out of the act. And later Zeppo did, too.

3. They began in vaudeville. That was before World War I. Their first show was called *I'll Say She Is*. It opened in New York in 1924.

NAME _____ DATE _____ SCORE _____

4. The Marx brothers' first movie was *The Coconuts*. The next was *Animal Crackers*. And this was followed by *Monkey Business, Horsefeathers,* and *Duck Soup*. Then came *A Night at the Opera*.

5. In each of these movies, the Marx brothers make people laugh. They also establish a unique, zany comic style.

6. In their movies, each man has a set of familiar trademarks. Groucho has a mustache and a long coat. He wiggles his eyebrows and smokes a cigar. There is a funny hat that Chico always wears. And he affects a phony Italian accent. Harpo never speaks.

NAME _____ DATE _____ SCORE _____

7. Groucho is always cast as a sly operator: He always tries to cheat people out of their money. He always tries to charm women.

8. In *The Coconuts* he plays Mr. Hammer, proprietor of the run-down Coconut Manor, a Florida hotel. In *Horsefeathers* his character is named Professor Quincy Adams Wagstaff. Wagstaff is president of Huxley College. Huxley also has financial problems.

9. In *Duck Soup* Groucho plays Rufus T. Firefly, president of the country of Fredonia. Fredonia was formerly ruled by the late husband of a Mrs. Teasdale. Fredonia is now at war with the country of Sylvania.

Copyright © 1998 by Harcourt Brace & Company. All rights reserved.

NAME _____ DATE _____ SCORE _____

10. Margaret Dumont is often Groucho's leading lady. She plays Mrs. Teasdale in *Duck Soup*. In *A Night at the Opera* she plays Mrs. Claypool. Her character in *The Coconuts* is named Mrs. Potter.

NAME _____ DATE _____ SCORE _____

EXERCISE 68: Correcting Faulty Parallelism

Identify and correct faulty parallelism in these sentences. Then underline the parallel elements—words, phrases, and clauses—in your corrected sentences. If a sentence is already correct, mark it with a C and underline the parallel elements.

EXAMPLE: Alfred Hitchcock's films include *North by Northwest*, *Vertigo*, *Psycho*, and he also directed *Notorious* and *Saboteur*.

REVISED: Films directed by Alfred Hitchcock include <u>*North by Northwest*</u>, <u>*Vertigo*</u>, <u>*Psycho*</u>, <u>*Notorious*</u> and <u>*Saboteur*</u>.

1. The world is divided between those with galoshes on and those who discover continents.

2. Soviet leaders, members of Congress, and the American Catholic bishops all pressed the president to limit the arms race.

NAME _____ DATE _____ SCORE _____

3. A national task force on education recommended improving public education by making the school day longer, higher teachers' salaries, and integrating more technology into the curriculum.

4. The fast-food industry is expanding to include many kinds of restaurants: those that serve pizza, fried chicken chains, some offering Mexican-style menus, and hamburger franchises.

5. The consumption of Scotch in the United States is declining because of high prices, tastes are changing, and increased health awareness has led many whiskey drinkers to switch to wine or beer.

6. With summer just around the corner, I'm looking forward to swimming in our pool, fishing at the lake, and we'll grill in our back yard.

NAME _____ DATE _____ SCORE _____

7. Brian has developed a challenging training program: before breakfast, he jogs; after lunch, he bikes; and after supper, swimming is his preference.

NAME _____ DATE _____ SCORE _____

EXERCISE 69: Identifying Headwords

In the following sentence pairs, the modifier in each sentence points to a different headword. Underline the modifier and draw an arrow to the word it limits. Then explain the meaning of each sentence.

EXAMPLE: She <u>just</u> →came in wearing a hat. (She just now entered.)

She came in wearing <u>just</u> →a hat. (She wore only a hat.)

1. He wore his almost new jeans.

   He almost wore his new jeans.

2. He only had three dollars in his pocket.

   Only he had three dollars in his pocket.

NAME _____ DATE _____ SCORE _____

3. I don't even like freshwater fish.

   I don't like even freshwater fish.

4. I go only to the beach on Saturdays.

   I go to the beach only on Saturdays.

5. He simply hated living.

   He hated simply living.

6. Not all of the information is printed clearly.

   All of the information is not printed clearly.

EXERCISE 70: Connecting Modifiers and Headwords

Underline the modifying verbal or prepositional phrases in each sentence and draw arrows to their headwords.

EXAMPLE: Calvin is the Democrat <u>running for town council.</u>

1. The bridge across the river swayed in the wind.

2. The spectators on the shore viewed in disbelief.

3. Mesmerized by the spectacle, they watched the drama unfold.

4. In unison, the spectators feared a disaster was certain.

5. Within the hour, the state police arrived to save the day.

6. They closed off the area with roadblocks.

7. Drivers approaching the bridge were asked to stop.

8. Meanwhile, on the bridge, the scene was chaos.

9. Motorists in their cars sat paralyzed with fear.

10. Struggling against the weather, the police managed to rescue everyone.

NAME _____ DATE _____ SCORE _____

11. A newspaper reporter, holding her camera, ran to a telephone at a nearby market.

12. Close to exhaustion, she reported the events to her editor.

NAME _____ DATE _____ SCORE _____

EXERCISE 71: Relocating Misplaced Modifiers

Relocate the misplaced verbal or prepositional phrases or dependent clauses so that they clearly point to the words or word groups they modify.

EXAMPLE: *Silent Running* is a film about a scientist left alone in space with Bruce Dern.

Silent Running is a film with Bruce Dern about a scientist left alone in space.

1. She realized that she had married the wrong man after the wedding.

2. *The Prince and the Pauper* is a novel about an exchange of identities by Mark Twain.

NAME _____ DATE _____ SCORE _____

3. The energy was used up in the ten-kilometer race that he was saving for the marathon.

4. He loaded the bottles and cans into his new Porsche, which he planned to leave at the recycling center.

5. The manager explained the sales figures to the board members using a graph.

6. The replacement door was delivered to my mother painted from top to bottom.

NAME _____ DATE _____ SCORE _____

EXERCISE 72: Relocating Misplaced Modifiers

Revise these sentences, so the modifying phrases or clauses do not interrupt the parts of a verb phrase or infinitive or separate a subject from a verb or a verb from its object or complement.

EXAMPLE: A play can sometimes be, despite the playwright's best efforts, mystifying to the audience.

Despite the playwright's best efforts, a play can sometimes be mystifying to the audience.

1. The people in the audience, when they saw the play was about to begin and realized the orchestra had finished tuning up and had begun the overture, finally quieted down.

2. They settled into their seats, expecting to very much enjoy the first act.

NAME _____ DATE _____ SCORE _____

3. However, most people were, even after watching and listening for twenty minutes and paying close attention to the drama, completely baffled.

4. In fact, the play, because it had nameless characters, no scenery, and a rambling plot that didn't seem to be heading anywhere, puzzled even the drama critics.

5. Finally one of the three major characters explained, speaking directly to the audience, what the play was really about.

NAME _____ DATE _____ SCORE _____

EXERCISE 73: Eliminating Dangling Modifiers

A. Eliminate the dangling modifier from each of the following sentences.

THEN

B. Supply a word or word group that the dangling modifier can logically modify.

OR

C. Change the dangling modifier into a dependent clause.

EXAMPLE: Skiing down the mountain, the restaurant seemed warm and inviting (dangling modifier)

Skiing down the mountain; I thought the restaurant seemed warm and inviting. (logical headword added)

<u>As I skied down the mountain,</u> the restaurant seemed warm and inviting. (dependent clause)

1. Although architecturally unusual, most people agree that Buckminster Fuller's geodesic dome is well designed.

NAME _____ DATE _____ SCORE _____

2. As an out-of-state student without a car, it was difficult to get to off-campus cultural events.

3. To build a campfire, kindling is necessary.

4. With every step upward, the trees became sparser.

5. Being an amateur tennis player, my backhand is weaker than my forehand.

6. When exiting the train, the station will be on your right.

7. Driving through the Mojave, the bleak landscape was oppressive.

8. By requiring auto manufacturers to further improve emission-control devices, the air quality will get better.

9. Using a piece of filter paper, the ball of sodium is dried as much as possible and placed in a test tube.

10. Having missed work for seven days straight, my job was in jeopardy.

Copyright © 1998 by Harcourt Brace & Company. All rights reserved.

NAME _____ DATE _____ SCORE _____

11. Having prepared a romantic candlelight dinner, the telephone was unplugged so we could enjoy the meal without interruption.

12. While running laps at the track each afternoon, my car is parked in front of the gym.

13. Walking into the dentist's office, the sound of the drill made my heartbeat race.

NAME _____ DATE _____ SCORE _____

EXERCISE 74: Level of Diction

After reading the following paragraphs, underline the words and phrases that identify each as formal diction. Then choose one paragraph and rewrite it using a level of diction that you would use in your college writing. Use a dictionary if necessary.

1. In looking at many small points of difference between species, which, as far as our ignorance permits us to judge, seem quite unimportant, we must not forget that climate, food, etc., have no doubt produced some direct effect. It is also necessary to bear in mind that owing to the law of correlation, when one part varies and the variations are accumulated through natural selection, other modifications, often of the most unexpected nature, will ensue. (Charles Darwin, *The Origin of Species*)

2. I hope you are able to see the distinction I am trying to point out. In no sense do I advocate evading or defying the law, as would the rabid segregationist. That would lead to anarchy. One

NAME _____ DATE _____ SCORE _____

who breaks an unjust law must do so openly, lovingly, and with a willingness to accept penalty. I submit that an individual who breaks a law that conscience tells him is unjust, and who willingly accepts the penalty of imprisonment in order to arouse the conscience of the community over its injustice, is in reality expressing the highest respect for law. (Martin Luther King, Jr., "Letter from Birmingham Jail")

NAME _____ DATE _____ SCORE _____

EXERCISE 75: General and Specific; Abstract and Concrete

Below is a paragraph taken from a letter designed to accompany a job application. Revise the paragraph by substituting specific, concrete language for general or abstract words and phrases.

    I have had several part-time jobs lately. Some of them would qualify me for the position you advertised. In my most recent job, I sold products in a store. My supervisor said I was a good worker who possessed a number of valuable qualities. I am used to dealing with different types of people in different types of settings. I feel that my qualifications would make me a good candidate for your job.

NAME _____ DATE _____ SCORE _____

EXERCISE 76: Denotation and Connotation

The following words have negative connotations. For each, list one word with a similar meaning whose connotation is neutral and another whose connotation is favorable.

EXAMPLE:

	Negative	*Neutral*	*Favorable*
	skinny	thin	slender

1. deceive

2. antiquated

3. egghead

4. pathetic

5. cheap

6. blunder

7. weird

8. politician

NAME _____ DATE _____ SCORE _____

9. shack

10. stench

11. swipe

12. treason

13. destroy

NAME _____ DATE _____ SCORE _____

EXERCISE 77: Denotation and Connotation

Think of a trip you took. First, write a one-sentence description that would discourage anyone from taking the same trip. Next, rewrite this sentence, describing your trip favorably. Finally, rewrite your sentence again, using neutral words that convey no judgments. In all three versions of your sentence, underline the words that helped you to convey your impressions to your readers.

NAME _____ DATE _____ SCORE _____

EXERCISE 78: Figures of Speech

Read the following paragraph from Mark Twain's *Life on the Mississippi* and identify as many figures of speech as you can.

    Now when I had mastered the language of this water, and had come to know every trifling feature that bordered the great river as familiarly as I knew the letters of the alphabet, I had made a valuable acquisition. But I had lost something, too. I had lost something which could never be restored to me while I lived. All the grace, the beauty, the poetry, had gone out of the majestic river! I still keep in mind a certain wonderful sunset which I witnessed when steamboating was new to me. A broad expanse of the river was turned to blood; in the middle distance the red hue brightened into gold, through which a solitary log came floating black and conspicuous; in one place a long, slanting mark lay sparkling upon the water; in another the surface was broken by boiling, tumbling rings, that were as many-tinted as an opal; where the ruddy flush was faintest, was a smooth spot that was covered

NAME _____ DATE _____ SCORE _____

with graceful circles and radiating lines, ever so delicately traced; the shore on our left was densely wooded, and the somber shadow that fell from this forest was broken in one place by a long, ruffled trail that shone like silver; and high above the forest wall a clean-stemmed dead tree waved a single leafy bough that glowed like a flame in the unobstructed splendor that was flowing from the sun. There were graceful curves, reflected images, woody heights, soft distances; and over the whole scene, far and near, the dissolving lights drifted steadily, enriching it every passing moment with new marvels of coloring.

simile(s)   **metaphor(s)**

personification(s)   **other figures**

NAME _____ DATE _____ SCORE _____

EXERCISE 79: Figures of Speech

Rewrite the following sentences, adding one figure of speech to each sentence to make the ideas more vivid and exciting.

Identify each figure of speech you use.

EXAMPLE: The room was cool and still.

                The room was cool and still like the inside of a cathedral. (simile)

1. The child was small and carelessly groomed.

2. I wanted to live life to its fullest.

3. The December morning was bright and cloudy.

4. As I walked I saw a cloud floating in the sky.

5. House cats stalk their prey.

6. The sunset turned the lake red.

7. The street was quiet except at the hour when the school at the corner let out.

Copyright © 1998 by Harcourt Brace & Company. All rights reserved.

NAME _____ DATE _____ SCORE _____

8. A shopping mall is a place where teenagers like to gather.

9. The president faced an angry Senate.

10. Education is a long process that takes much hard work.

NAME _____ DATE _____ SCORE _____

EXERCISE 80: Eliminating Biased Language

Identify the stereotypes in the following sentences:

1. Uncle Max wasn't surprised to find that the driver of the car that rear ended his new BMW was a woman.

2. A new medical school student knows that he faces several years of hard work.

3. California has a large Oriental population.

4. She couldn't wait to leave her hometown because it was populated with rednecks and hicks.

5. Because of a back injury, he was confined to a wheelchair.

6. I was surprised to notice that my hairdresser wears a wedding ring.

7. My roommate was born and raised in Tennessee, but he surprises me by wearing shoes to class.

8. Next Tuesday is her day to have the girls over for bridge.

NAME _____ DATE _____ SCORE _____

9. With a handwriting like that, you'll do great in pre-med.

10. She's a third-year engineering student, so I won't waste my time asking her to proofread my essay.

NAME _____ DATE _____ SCORE _____

EXERCISE 81: Gender-Neutral Alternatives

Suggest possible alternative forms for any of the following constructions you consider sexist. In each case, comment on the advantages and disadvantages of the alternative you recommend. If you feel that a particular term is not sexist, explain why.

forefathers

man-eating shark

manpower

workmen's compensation

men at work

copyboy

busboy

first baseman

corpsman

congressman

longshoreman

committeeman

(to) man the battle stations

girl Friday

NAME _____ DATE _____ SCORE _____

Board of Selectmen

stock boy

cowboy

man overboard

fisherman

foreman

NAME _____ DATE _____ SCORE _____

EXERCISE 82: Terms Denoting Professions

These terms denote professions that have traditionally been associated with a particular gender. Now that the professions are open to both sexes, are any new terms needed? If so, suggest possible terms. If not, explain why not.

miner

mechanic

soldier

sailor

rancher

farmer

barber

rabbi

minister

bartender

plumber

clergyman

fireman

policeman

EXERCISE 83: Gender-Neutral Coinages

The following terms have emerged in the last few years as possible alternatives for older gender-specific words. Which usages do you believe are likely to become part of the English language? Which do you expect to disappear? Explain.

Coinage	Older Form
• waitperson server	waiter or waitress
• househusband homemaker	housewife
• weather forecaster	weatherman, weathergirl
• chair chairwoman chairperson	chairman
• spokesperson	spokesman
• letter carrier	mailman

NAME _____ DATE _____ SCORE _____

EXERCISE 84: Masculine/Feminine Word Forms

Each of the following pairs of terms includes a feminine form that was at one time in wide use; all are still used to some extent. Which do you think are likely to remain in our language for some time, and which do you think will disappear? Explain your reasoning.

heir/heiress

benefactor/benefactress

murderer/murderess

actor/actress

hero/heroine

host/hostess

aviator/aviatrix

executor/executrix

author/authoress

poet/poetess

tailor/seamstress

comedian/comedienne

villain/villainess

prince/princess

widow/widower

EXERCISE 85: Grammatical Forms

Use your college dictionary to answer the following questions about grammatical form.

1. What are the principal parts of the following verbs: *drink, deify, carol, draw,* and *ring*?

2. Which of the following nouns can be used as verbs: *canter, minister, council, command, magistrate, mother,* and *lord*?

3. What are the plural forms of these nouns: *silo, sheep, seed, scissors, genetics,* and *alchemy*?

4. What are the comparative and superlative forms of the following adverbs and adjectives: *fast, airy, good, mere, homey,* and *unlucky*?

5. Are the following verbs transitive, intransitive, or both: *bias, halt, dissatisfy, die,* and *turn*? Copy the phrase or sentence from the dictionary that illustrates the use of each verb.

NAME _____ DATE _____ SCORE _____

EXERCISE 86: Usage Restrictions

Use your college dictionary to find the restrictions on the use of the following words.

1. irregardless

2. apse

3. flunk

4. lorry

5. kirk

6. gofer

7. whilst

8. sine

9. bannock

10. blowhard

NAME _____ DATE _____ SCORE _____

EXERCISE 87: Research Capabilities

To test the research capability of your dictionary, use it to answer the following questions.

1. In what year did Anwar el-Sadat win the Nobel Peace Prize?

2. After whom was the Ferris wheel named?

3. What is the atomic weight of sulfur?

4. What was Joseph Conrad's original name?

5. What is surrealism?

Copyright © 1998 by Harcourt Brace & Company. All rights reserved.

NAME _____ DATE _____ SCORE _____

EXERCISE 88: Histories of Words

Using your college dictionary, look up the etymologies of the following words. How does the history of each word help you remember its definition?

1. mountebank

2. pyrrhic

3. pittance

4. protean

5. gargantuan

6. cicerone

7. fathom

8. gossamer

9. rigmarole

10. maudlin

NAME _____ DATE _____ SCORE _____

EXERCISE 89: Periods

Correct these sentences by adding missing periods and deleting unnecessary ones. If a sentence is correct, write *correct*.

EXAMPLE: Dr. Toly will discuss neuropsychology during Grand Rounds at 7:30 p.m.

   Dr. Toly will discuss neuropsychology during Grand Rounds at 7:30 p.m.

1. Students are sometimes confused by the difference between B.C.E. and C.E.

2. Having gone through rigorous training, they were prepared now for their work in the Peace Corps

3. Have most of the faculty earned the M.A.?

4. After she graduated from USC with a J.D, she interviewed with the F.B.I.

5. The President's press conference at D.O.E. was scheduled for 10 am, but it was postponed until 2 p.m.

NAME _____ DATE _____ SCORE _____

EXERCISE 90: Question Marks

Correct the use of question marks and other punctuation in the following sentences.

EXAMPLE: She asked whether Freud's theories were accepted during his lifetime?

She asked whether Freud's theories were accepted during his lifetime.

1. He wondered whether he should take a nine o'clock class?

2. The instructor asked, "Was the Spanish-American War a victory for America?"?

3. Are they really going to China??!!

4. He took a modest (?) portion of dessert—half a pie.

5. "Is *data* the plural of *datum*?," he inquired.

NAME _____ DATE _____ SCORE _____

EXERCISE 91: Exclamation Points

Correct the use of exclamation points and other punctuation in these sentences.

EXAMPLE: "My God," she cried. "I've been shot!!!"

"My God," she cried. "I've been shot!"

1. Are you kidding?! I never said that.

2. When the cell divided, each of the daughter cells had an extra chromosome!

3. This is fantastic. I can't believe you bought this for me.

4. Wow!! Just what I always wanted!! A pink Cadillac!!

5. "Eureka!," cried Archimedes as he sprang from his bathtub.

NAME _____ DATE _____ SCORE _____

EXERCISE 92: Review of End Punctuation

Add appropriate punctuation to this passage. Write your changes between the lines.

Dr Craig and his group of divers paused at the shore, staring respectfully at the enormous lake Who could imagine what terrors lay beneath its surface Which of them might not emerge alive from this adventure Would it be Col Cathcart Capt Wilks, the MD from the naval base Her husband, P L Fox Or would they all survive the task ahead Dr Craig decided some encouraging remarks were in order

"Attention divers," he said in a loud, forceful voice "May I please have your attention The project which we are about to undertake—"

"Oh, no" screamed Mr Fox suddenly "Look out It's the Loch Ness Monster"

"Quick" shouted Dr Craig "Move away from the shore" But his warning came too late

NAME _____ DATE _____ SCORE _____

EXERCISE 93: Commas in Compound Sentences

Combine each of the following sentence pairs into one compound sentence, using the coordinating conjunction in parentheses. Add commas where necessary.

EXAMPLE: Bird watching in exotic places is a popular activity. I like watching the ordinary varieties in my back yard. (but)

Bird watching in exotic places is a popular activity, but I like watching the ordinary varieties in my back yard.

1. Cross-country skiing was not her favorite activity. She did not enjoy downhill skiing. (nor)

2. Managed health care plans are less expensive than traditional fee-for-service plans. More employers are including them in the employee benefit package. (so)

3. For their 50th anniversary her parents were considering a trip to Indonesia. They might take a cruise around the Greek Isles. (or)

NAME _____ DATE _____ SCORE _____

4. Mt. Lemon is a ski area near Tucson, Arizona. Most visitors to Tucson come to enjoy the desert sun. (but)

5. Viatical insurance plans may be advantageous for people who are seriously ill. They may be lucrative financially for those who buy them from these seriously ill people. (and)

NAME _____ DATE _____ SCORE _____

EXERCISE 94: Commas to Separate Items in a Series

Insert and delete commas in the following sentences to properly separate items in a series. Mark *correct* if the sentence is correct.

EXAMPLE: Chickadees cardinals, chipping sparrows and house wrens use the tree in my back yard as their playground.

Chickadees, cardinals, chipping sparrows, and house wrens use the tree in my back yard as their playground.

1. Cholla, teddy bear prickly pear and saguaro are all cacti.

2. The National Park System is responsible for maintaining our national heritage safeguarding wildlife and providing positive visitor experiences.

3. The Grand Canyon is in Arizona, but Sequoia Yosemite and Death Valley are in California and Rocky Mountain and Mesa Verde National Parks are in Colorado.

4. Glacier Yosemite Yellowstone Grand Canyon, Great Smoky Mountains and Grand Tetons are all magnificent parks in the United States.

5. National urban treasures include the Statue of Liberty in New York, and the Lincoln Memorial, the Washington Monument, and the Jefferson Memorial in Washington, DC.

NAME _____ DATE _____ SCORE _____

EXERCISE 95: Commas to Separate Coordinate Adjectives

Add two coordinate adjectives to modify each of the following combinations, inserting commas where required.

EXAMPLE: classical music
strong, beautiful classical music

1. distant thunder

2. silver spoon

3. New York Yankees

4. miniature golf

5. Rolling Stones

6. loving couple

7. computer science

8. wheat bread

9. art museum

10. new math

NAME _____ DATE _____ SCORE _____

EXERCISE 96: Commas to Set Off Introductory Elements

Add commas in this paragraph where they are needed to set off an introductory element from the rest of the sentence. Write your changes between the lines.

When the most sagacious of Victorian culinarians, Mrs. Beeton, spoke rather cryptically of the "alliaceous tribe" she was referring to none other than the ancient and noble members of the lily family known in kitchens round the world as the onion, scallion, leek, shallot, clove, and garlic. I don't suppose it really matters that many cooks today are hardly aware of the close affinity the common bulb onion we take so much for granted has with these other vegetables of the *Allium* genus, but it does bother me how Americans underestimate the versatility of the onion and how so few give a second thought to exploiting the potential of its

NAME _____ DATE _____ SCORE _____

aromatic relatives. More often than not the onion itself is considered no more than a flavoring agent to soups, stews, stocks, sauces, salads, and sandwiches. Though I'd be the last to deny that nothing awakens the gustatory senses or inspires the soul like the aroma of onions simmering in a lusty stew or the crunch of a few sweet, odoriferous slices on a juicy hamburger it would be nice to see the onion highlighted in ways other than the all-too-familiar fried rings and creamed preparations. (James Villas, "E Pluribus Onion")

NAME _____ DATE _____ SCORE _____

EXERCISE 97: Commas to Set Off Nonrestrictive Elements

Insert commas where necessary to set off nonrestrictive phrases and clauses. Write your changes between the lines.

The Statue of Liberty which was dedicated in 1886 has undergone extensive renovation. Its supporting structure whose designer was the French engineer Alexandre Gustave Eiffel is made of iron. The Statue of Liberty created over a period of nine years by sculptor Frédéric-Auguste Bartholdi stands 151 feet tall. The people of France who were grateful for American help in the French Revolution raised the money to pay the sculptor who created the statue. The people of the United States contributing over $100,000 raised the money for the pedestal on which the statue stands.

NAME _____ DATE _____ SCORE _____

EXERCISE 98: Commas to Set Off Nonessential Elements

Set off the nonessential elements in these sentences with commas, as shown below. If a sentence is correct, mark it with a C in the left margin.

EXAMPLE: Piranhas like sharks will attack and eat almost anything if the opportunity arises.

Piranhas,^ like sharks,^ will attack and eat almost anything if the opportunity arises.

1. Kermit the Frog is a muppet a cross between a marionette and a puppet.

2. The common cold a virus is frequently spread by hand contact not by mouth.

3. The account in the Bible of Noah's Ark and the forty-day flood may be based on an actual deluge.

4. More than two-thirds of U.S. welfare recipients, such as children, the aged, the severely disabled, and mothers of children under six, are people with legitimate reasons for not working.

5. The submarine *Nautilus* was the first to cross under the North Pole wasn't it?

6. The 1958 Ford Edsel was advertised with the slogan "Once you've seen it, you'll never forget it."

NAME _____ DATE _____ SCORE _____

7. Superman was called Kal-El on the planet Krypton; on earth however he was known as Clark Kent not Kal-El.

8. Its sales topping any of his previous singles "Heartbreak Hotel" was Elvis Presley's first million seller.

9. Two companies Nash and Hudson joined in 1954 to form American Motors.

10. A firefly is a beetle not a fly and a prairie dog is a rodent not a dog.

NAME _____ DATE _____ SCORE _____

EXERCISE 99: Commas to Set Off Quotations, Names, Dates, Etc.

Add commas (‸) where necessary to set off quotations, names, dates, addresses, and numbers.

1. India became independent on August 15 1947.

2. The UAW has more than 1500000 dues-paying members.

3. Nikita Khrushchev, former Soviet premier, said "We will bury you!"

4. Mount St. Helens, northeast of Portland Oregon, began erupting on March 27 1980 and eventually killed at least thirty people.

5. Located at 1600 Pennsylvania Avenue Washington D.C., the White House is a popular tourist attraction.

6. In 1956, playing before a crowd of 64519 fans in Yankee Stadium in New York New York, Don Larsen pitched the first perfect game in World Series history.

7. Lewis Thomas M.D. was born in Flushing New York and attended Harvard Medical School in Cambridge Massachusetts.

8. In 1967 2000000 people worldwide died of smallpox, but in 1977 only about twenty died.

NAME _____ DATE _____ SCORE _____

9. "The reports of my death" Mark Twain remarked "have been greatly exaggerated."

10. The French explorer Jean Nicolet landed at Green Bay Wisconsin in 1634, and in 1848 Wisconsin became the thirtieth state; it has 10355 lakes and a population of more than 4700000.

EXERCISE 100: Commas to Prevent Misreading

Insert commas to prevent reader confusion. Mark any sentence that is correct with a *C*.

EXAMPLE: In America's adolescence freak shows were commonplace.

In America's adolescence, freak shows were commonplace.

1. According to Mitsuoko Kim's spoken English is excellent.

2. Lina flew Air Afrique; Molly, Lufthansa.

3. By talking passengers might control their fear of flying.

4. My mother always tells me, "When driving drive safely."

5. Our airline snack consisted of a stale bun with dry meat and flavorless cookies.

NAME _____ DATE _____ SCORE _____

EXERCISE 101: Review of Commas

Commas have been intentionally deleted from some of the following sentences. Add commas (⌃) where needed, and be prepared to explain why each is necessary. If a sentence is correct, mark it with a *C* in the left margin.

1. Sometimes they did go shopping or to a movie but sometimes they went across the highway ducking fast across the busy road to a drive-in restaurant where older kids hung out. The restaurant was shaped like a big bottle though squatter than a real bottle and on its cap was a revolving figure of a grinning boy who held a hamburger aloft. (Joyce Carol Oates, "Where Are You Going, Where Have You Been?")

2. His head whirled as he stepped into the thronged corridor and he sank back into one of the chairs against the wall to get his breath. The lights the chatter the perfumes the bewildering medley of color—he had for a moment the feeling of not being able to stand it. (Willa Cather, "Paul's Case")

3. It has been longed for campaigned for kissed and caressed on the top of its shiny 24-karat-gold-plated bald head. It has inspired giddiness wordiness speechlessness glee, and—in the case of the stars it has eluded—reactions ranging from wonder to rage. (*Life*, in an article about the Oscar)

4. Yes society often did treat the elderly abysmally . . . they were sometimes ignored sometimes victimized sometimes poor and frightened but so many of them were survivors. (Katherine Barrett, "Old Before Her Time")

NAME _____ DATE _____ SCORE _____

5. The word success comes from the Latin verb *succedere* meaning "to follow after." (Susan Ochshorn, "Economic Adventurers")

6. It was a big squarish frame house that had once been white decorated with cupolas and spires and scrolled balconies in the heavily lightsome style of the seventies set on what had once been our most select street. (William Faulkner, "A Rose for Emily")

7. The world as always is debating the issues of war and peace. (Sam Keen, "Faces of the Enemy")

8. About fifteen miles below Monterey on the wild coast the Torres family had their farm a few sloping acres above a cliff that dropped to the brown reefs and to the hissing white waters of the ocean. (John Steinbeck, "Flight")

9. I was looking for myself and asking everyone except myself questions which I and only I could answer. (Ralph Ellison, *Invisible Man*)

10. According to the Pet Food Institute a Washington-based trade association there were about 18 million more dogs than cats in the United States as recently as a decade ago but today there are 56 million cats and only 52 million dogs. (Cullen Murphy, "Going to the Cats")

NAME _____ DATE _____ SCORE _____

EXERCISE 102: Punctuation to Separate Independent Clauses

Add semicolons, periods, or commas plus coordinating conjunctions where necessary to separate independent clauses. Reread the paragraph when you have finished to make certain no comma splices or fused sentences remain.

EXAMPLE: *Birth of a Nation* was one of the earliest epic movies it was based on the book *The Klansman.*

Birth of a Nation was one of the earliest epic movies^; it was based on the book *The Klansman.*

During the 1950s movie attendance declined because of the increasing popularity of television. As a result, numerous gimmicks were introduced to draw audiences into theaters. One of the first of these was Cinerama, in this technique three pictures were shot side by side and projected on a curved screen. Next came 3-D, complete with special glasses, *Bwana Devil* and *The Creature from the Black Lagoon* were two

NAME _____ DATE _____ SCORE _____

early 3-D ventures. *The Robe* was the first picture filmed in Cinemascope in this technique a shrunken image was projected on a screen twice as wide as it was tall. Smell-O-Vision (or Aromarama) was a short-lived gimmick that enabled audiences to smell what they were viewing problems developed when it became impossible to get one odor out of the theater in time for the next smell to be introduced. William Castle's *Thirteen Ghosts* introduced special glasses for cowardly viewers who wanted to be able to control what they saw, the red part of the glasses was the "ghost viewer" and the green part was the "ghost remover." Perhaps the ultimate in movie gimmicks accompanied the film *The Tingler* when this film was shown seats in the theater were wired to generate mild electric shocks. Unfortunately, the shocks set off

NAME _____ DATE _____ SCORE _____

a chain reaction that led to hysteria in the theater. During the 1960s such gimmicks all but disappeared, viewers were able once again to simply sit back and enjoy a movie.

NAME _____ DATE _____ SCORE _____

EXERCISE 103: Semicolons to Separate Independent Clauses

Combine each of the following sentence groups into one sentence that contains only two independent clauses. Use a semicolon to separate the two clauses. You may need to add, delete, relocate, or change some words; keep experimenting until you find the arrangement that best conveys the meaning of the group of sentences. Your answers may vary from the model answer.

EXAMPLE: In the springtime, birds nest in the fir tree in my back yard. I see fluttering chickadees. I see bold cardinals.

In the springtime, birds nest in the fir tree in my back yard; I see fluttering chickadees and bold cardinals.

1. Television soap operas provide a diversion to real life. Soap opera characters are always wealthy. They never seem to work.

2. Ads on afternoon soap operas are directed primarily toward women. The viewer rarely sees ads for men on afternoon soap operas. These ads include soap, toothpaste, skin creams, and nail products.

NAME _____ DATE _____ SCORE _____

3. Hale-Bopp was an extraordinary comet. It was seen by millions of ordinary people. It was visible at sunrise and sunset in the spring of 1997 throughout the United States.

4. In many places in the United States, the legal system finds it difficult to try rape cases. Victims feel shame. They are embarrassed to testify.

5. I looked for an article on babies born addicted to cocaine. I looked for a long time. The article was hard to find. It was quite useful.

6. On the bottom of the shelf sits an almost obsolete, yet once expensive, turntable. Next to it are a dusty 8-track player and large speakers. Across the room in a prominent position on the entertainment center resides a gleaming CD player.

7. The United States Capitol is at one end of the Mall. The Washington Monument is at the other end. The space in-between is used by both visitors and residents for volleyball, sunbathing, and strolling.

NAME _____ DATE _____ SCORE _____

EXERCISE 104: Sentence Combining

Combine each of the following sentence groups into one sentence that contains only two independent clauses. Use a semicolon and the conjunctive adverb or transitional phrase in parentheses to join the two clauses, adding commas within clauses where necessary. You will need to add, delete, locate, or change some words. There is no one correct version; keep experimenting until you find the arrangement you feel is most effective.

EXAMPLE: There has been a sharp increase in vulgar language in high school essays. Teachers say they can't ignore it. Teachers will begin classroom instruction to combat the problem. (Therefore)

There has been a sharp increase in vulgar language in high school essays which teachers say they can't ignore; therefore, they will begin classroom instruction to combat the problem.

1. Teachers will instruct students on differences between formal and casual language. Teachers will give writing assignments requiring formal language. The purpose is not to destroy the language that students use. (However)

NAME _____ DATE _____ SCORE _____

2. The purpose is to make students more versatile in language use. Students should be able to write essay tests, short answer tests, and full-length compositions. They also should be able to do professional writing such as résumés and job applications. (For example)

3. Some students think that the whole idea is silly. Some students think talking about language is a waste of time. Sixteen-year-old Marta Sharif said they could use some lessons in language courtesy. (Still)

4. Marta continued. She said she gets tired of hearing foul language. She said she hears this language frequently as she walks across campus. (Unfortunately)

5. Her parents are appalled at the language they hear from young people in public. They support the school's efforts. They would like to see the efforts go further. (In fact)

NAME _____ DATE _____ SCORE _____

EXERCISE 105: Semicolons to Separate Items in a Series

Where necessary, replace commas with semicolons to separate internally punctuated items in a series.

EXAMPLE: The birds in the trees outside my window amuse me because they bicker cheerfully, because they swoop merrily through the air, and because they hop perkily from branch to branch.

The birds in the trees outside my window amuse me because they bicker cheerfully; because they swoop merrily through the air; and because they hop perkily from branch to branch.

1. Margaret Atwood wrote *Lady Oracle*, which is about the life crisis of a middle-aged woman, *The Robber Bride*, which humorously tells the age-old story of women and men, and *Alias Grace*, which is a fictionalized account of a real-life, nineteenth-century murder.

2. A new, inexpensive automobile has several advantages for a college student: the monthly payments will be low, which is especially important for the budget, it won't require costly repairs, which usually are needed at the worst possible moment, and, after graduation, it can be used as a down payment on a newer model.

NAME _____ DATE _____ SCORE _____

3. Properly prescribed antidepressants, such as Prozac and Paxil, may benefit the patient by easing anxiety, therefore allowing the person to concentrate better, by improving sleep patterns, which is especially important for people who must mentally focus on important tasks, and by moderating the sometimes severe blue moods of depression.

4. Both high school and college students may use the term "geek" to describe an extremely bright, socially unskilled person, "nerd" to describe someone neither bright, socially skilled, nor well-dressed, and "jock" to describe the muscular, athletic, usually non-academically oriented student.

5. The process of registering for college is often a hassle, requiring a student to stand seemingly for hours in long, curving lines, to fill out endless, meaningless forms, and to walk from building to building in search of the right advisor to sign those forms.

NAME _____ DATE _____ SCORE _____

EXERCISE 106: Sentence Combining

Combine each of the following sentence groups into one sentence that includes a series of items separated by semicolons. You will need to add, delete, relocate, or change words. Try several versions of each sentence until you find the most effective arrangement. Write in the spaces provided.

EXAMPLE: Collecting baseball cards is a worthwhile hobby. It helps children learn how to bargain and trade. It also encourages them to assimilate, evaluate, and compare data about major league ball players. Perhaps most important, it encourages them to find role models in the athletes whose cards they collect.

Collecting baseball cards is a worthwhile hobby because it helps children learn how to bargain and trade; encourages them to assimilate, evaluate, and compare data about major league ball players; and, perhaps most important, encourages them to find role models in the athletes whose cards they collect.

1. A good dictionary offers definitions of words, including some obsolete and nonstandard words. It provides information about synonyms, usage, and word origins. It also offers information on pronunciation and syllabication.

NAME _____ DATE _____ SCORE _____

2. The flags of the Scandinavian countries all depict a cross on a solid background. Denmark's flag is red with a white cross. Norway's flag is also red, but its cross is blue, outlined in white. Sweden's flag is blue with a yellow cross.

3. Over one hundred international collectors' clubs are thriving today. One of these associations is the Cola Clan, whose members buy, sell, and trade Coca-Cola memorabilia. Another is the Citrus Label Society. There is also a Cookie Cutter Collectors' Club.

4. Listening to the radio special, we heard "Shuffle Off to Buffalo" and "Moon over Miami," both of which are about eastern cities. We heard "By the Time I Get to Phoenix" and "I Left My Heart in San Francisco," which mention western cities. Finally, we heard "The Star-Spangled Banner," which seemed to be an appropriate finale.

NAME _____ DATE _____ SCORE _____

5. There are three principal types of contact lenses. Hard contact lenses, also called conventional lenses, are easy to clean and handle and quite sturdy. Soft lenses, which are easily contaminated and must be cleaned and disinfected daily, are less durable. Gas-permeable lenses, sometimes advertised as semihard or semisoft lenses, look and feel like hard lenses but are more easily contaminated and less durable.

NAME _____ DATE _____ SCORE _____

EXERCISE 107: Review of Semicolons

Read this paragraph carefully. Then add semicolons where necessary and delete excess or incorrectly used ones, substituting other punctuation where necessary. Write your changes between the lines.

Barnstormers were aviators; who toured the country after World War I, giving people short airplane rides and exhibitions of stunt flying, in fact the name *barnstormer* was derived from the use of barns as airplane hangars. Americans' interest in airplanes had all but disappeared after the war; planes had served their function in battle, but when the war ended, most people saw no future in aviation. The barnstormers helped popularize flying; especially in rural areas. Some of them were pilots who had flown in the war; others were just young men with a thirst for adventure. They gave people rides in airplanes; sometimes charging a dollar a minute.

NAME _____ DATE _____ SCORE _____

For most passengers, this was their first ride in an airplane, in fact, sometimes it was their first sight of one. In the early 1920s, people grew bored with what the barnstormers had to offer; so groups of pilots began to stage spectacular—but often dangerous—stunt shows. Then, after Lindbergh's 1927 flight across the Atlantic; Americans suddenly needed no encouragement to embrace aviation. The barnstormers had outlived their usefulness; and an era ended. (Adapted from William Goldman, *Adventures in the Screen Trade*)

NAME _____ DATE _____ SCORE _____

EXERCISE 108: Possessives

Change the modifying phrases that following the nouns to possessive forms that precede the nouns.

1. the flights of American Airlines

2. the briefs of the attorney

3. the children of Mrs. Irie

4. the classes Janna Deppas takes

5. the speech by Ricardo Ortiz

6. the iguanas owned by Nicole Baday

7. the sweater belonging to Mulu Menshu

8. the nanny whom Judy and her husband hired

9. the many unique designs of Thomas Jefferson

10. the dinner given by supporters of the President

NAME _____ DATE _____ SCORE _____

EXERCISE 109: Possessives

Change the word or words in parentheses to possessive form.

EXAMPLE: (Susan) cat Indy likes to sit on top of her computer.

   Susan's cat Indy likes to sit on top of her computer.

1. (Delta Airlines) routes are worldwide.

2. (John Adams) contributions to the transition of the United States from colony to self-government are sometimes under appreciated.

3. (Stephen King) and (Danielle Steel) novels are perfect for summer vacation reading.

4. (Phoenix) Desert Museum highlights (visitors) sightseeing excursions.

5. (T.V. s) graphic violence and sex are under scrutiny by politicians and the public.

Copyright © 1998 by Harcourt Brace & Company. All rights reserved.

NAME _____ DATE _____ SCORE _____

EXERCISE 110: Plural Nouns or Possessive Pronouns

Correct any errors in the use of apostrophes to form plural nouns or to form the possessive case of personal pronouns. Some necessary apostrophes are omitted; other apostrophes are incorrectly inserted. Write *correct* if the sentence is correct.

EXAMPLE: Our migrating birds are the ones' that require winter feeding.

Our migrating birds are the ones that require winter feeding.

1. Ours are the ones you should be careful about.

2. Pacific Airlines seats seem adequate primarily for smaller passengers.

3. My parents' seats on Pacific Airlines' are two rows behind your's.

4. The popularity of cable television challenge's the three major networks' profits.

5. Potato chips and soft drinks' are a standard diet of her's.

6. Flight attendant's jobs are often hectic.

7. Many passengers ignore safety regulations' at the beginning of flights.

8. Geena Davis' role in *Earth Girls Are Easy* strengthened her acting credentials.

NAME _____ DATE _____ SCORE _____

9. *The Firm*, John Grishams novel, was made into a successful movie, as were several of his other books.

10. The City of Tucson's annexation of the Avra Road area is being fought by the residents.

NAME _____ DATE _____ SCORE _____

EXERCISE 111: Contractions

Correct any errors in the use of standard contractions or personal pronouns. If a sentence is correct, write *correct*.

EXAMPLE: The nesting birds in my back yard tree have found they're own little piece of heaven.

The nesting birds in my back yard tree have found their own little piece of heaven.

1. Who's movies do you think are better: Delta's or American's?

2. The pilot turned on the seat belt sign because its a rough flight.

3. If its much rougher, your going to spill your coffee.

4. Their trying to read the newspaper, but they're finding the airplane too bouncy.

5. Occasionally, your going to find it too rough even to hold your soft drink can without its spilling.

6. Who's coming with me to ask the gate agent about our next flight?

NAME _____ DATE _____ SCORE _____

7. "Our's is the flight to Taiwan," I said.

8. Having seen there hard work, I like to thank the flight attendants personally.

9. The special lunches were our's, but they were given to others.

10. Our landing at Heathrow Airport was smooth, but their was no gate agent to meet us.

NAME _____ DATE _____ SCORE _____

EXERCISE 112: Plurals of Letters and Numbers

Form correct plurals for the letters, numbers, and words in parentheses. Underline to indicate italics where necessary.

EXAMPLE: Mississippi is hard to spell because it has four (i), four (s), and two (p).

Mississippi is hard to spell because it has four *i*'s, four *s*'s, and two *p*'s.

1. In the game of tic-tac-toe, players line up (X) and (O) to win.

2. "They said they were (goin) to school, but I think they were just (playin) hooky!"

3. His writing incorporated many (prioritize), (parameter), and (indicator).

4. When I write (7) in the United States, they look different from my (7) when I'm in France; the same is true for (Z).

5. Most faculty have multiple degrees including (M.A.), (M.S.), and (M.F.A.).

NAME _____ DATE _____ SCORE _____

EXERCISE 113: Direct Quotations

Add single and double quotation marks to these sentences where necessary to set off direct quotations from identifying tags. If a sentence is correct, mark it with a C.

EXAMPLE: Wordsworth's phrase splendour in the grass was used as the title of a movie about young lovers.

Wordsworth's phrase "splendour in the grass" was used as the title of a movie about young lovers.

1. Mr. Fox noted, Few people can explain what Descartes' words I think, therefore I am actually mean.

2. Gertrude Stein said, You are all a lost generation.

3. Freedom of speech does not guarantee anyone the right to yell fire in a crowded theater, she explained.

4. Dorothy kept insisting that there was no place quite like home.

5. If everyone will sit down the teacher announced the exam will begin.

NAME _____ DATE _____ SCORE _____

EXERCISE 114: Titles and Words Used in a Special Sense

Add quotation marks to the following sentences where necessary to set off titles and words. If italics are incorrectly used, substitute quotation marks.

EXAMPLE: To Tim, social security means a date for Saturday night.

To Tim, "social security" means a date for Saturday night.

1. *First Fig* and *Second Fig* are two of the poems in Edna St. Vincent Millay's *Collected Poems*.

2. In the article Feminism Takes a New Turn, Betty Friedan reconsiders some of the issues first raised in her 1964 book *The Feminine Mystique*.

3. Edwin Arlington Robinson's poem Richard Cory was the basis for the song Richard Cory written by Paul Simon.

4. *Beside* means next to, but *besides* means except.

5. In an essay on the novel *An American Tragedy* published in *The Yale Review*, Robert Penn Warren noted, Theodore Dreiser once said that his philosophy of love might be called Varietism.

EXERCISE 115: Dialogue

Add appropriate quotation marks to the dialogue in this passage, beginning a new paragraph whenever a new speaker is introduced. Write in the space provided below.

The next time, the priest steered me into the confession box himself and left the shutter back [so] I could see him get in and sit down at the further side of the grille from me. Well, now, he said, what do they call you? Jackie, father, said I. And what's a-trouble to you, Jackie? Father, I said, feeling I might as well get it over while I had him in good humor, I had it all arranged to kill my grandmother.

NAME _____ DATE _____ SCORE _____

EXERCISE 116: Review of Quotation Marks

In the following paragraph, correct the use of single and double quotation marks to set off direct quotations, titles, and words used in a special sense. Supply the appropriate quotation marks where required and delete those not required. Be careful not to use quotation marks where they are not necessary. Write your changes between the lines.

In her essay 'The Obligation to Endure' from the book "Silent Spring," Rachel Carson writes: As Albert Schweitzer has said, 'Man can hardly even recognize the devils of his own creation.' Carson goes on to point out that many chemicals have been used to kill insects and other organisms which, she writes, are "described in the modern vernacular as pests." Carson believes such "advanced" chemicals, by contaminating our environment, do more harm than good. In addition to "Silent Spring," Carson is also the author of the book "The Sea Around

NAME _____ DATE _____ SCORE _____

Us." This work, divided into three sections (Mother Sea, The Restless Sea, and Man and the Sea About Him) was published in 1951.

NAME _____ DATE _____ SCORE _____

EXERCISE 117: Review of Quotation Marks

Correct the use of quotation marks in the following sentences, making sure that the use and placement of any accompanying punctuation marks are consistent with accepted conventions. Write your changes on or between the lines. If a sentence is correct, mark it with a C in the left margin.

EXAMPLE: The "Watergate" incident brought many new terms into the English language.

The Watergate incident brought many new terms into the English language.

1. Kilroy was here and Women and children first are two expressions that *Bartlett's Familiar Quotations* attributes to "Anon."

2. Neil Armstrong said he was making a small step for man but a giant leap for mankind.

3. "The answer, my friend", Bob Dylan sang, "is blowin' in the wind".

4. The novel was a real "thriller," complete with spies and counterspies, mysterious women, and exotic international chases.

5. The sign said, Road liable to subsidence; it meant that we should look out for potholes.

NAME _____ DATE _____ SCORE _____

6. One of William Blake's best-known lines—To see a world in a grain of sand—opens his poem Auguries of Innocence.

7. In James Thurber's short story The Catbird Seat, Mrs. Barrows annoys Mr. Martin by asking him silly questions like Are you tearing up the pea patch? Are you scraping around the bottom of the pickle barrel? and Are you lifting the oxcart out of the ditch?

8. I'll make him an offer he can't refuse, promised "the godfather" in Mario Puzo's novel.

9. What did Timothy Leary mean by "Turn on, tune in, drop out?"

10. George, the protagonist of Bernard Malamud's short story, A Summer's Reading, is something of an "underachiever."

Copyright © 1998 by Harcourt Brace & Company. All rights reserved.

NAME _____ DATE _____ SCORE _____

EXERCISE 118: Colons

Add colons where required in the following sentences. If necessary, delete excess colons.

EXAMPLE: There was one thing he really hated getting up at 700 every morning.

There was one thing he really hated: getting up at 7:00 every morning.

1. Books about the late John F. Kennedy include the following *A Hero for Our Time; Johnny We Hardly Knew Ye; One Brief Shining Moment;* and *JFK: Reckless Youth.*

2. Only one task remained to tell his boss he was quitting.

3. The story closed with a familiar phrase "And they all lived happily ever after."

4. The sergeant requested: reinforcements, medical supplies, and more ammunition.

5. She kept only four souvenirs a photograph, a matchbook, a theater program, and a daisy pressed between the pages of *William Shakespeare The Complete Works.*

NAME _____ DATE _____ SCORE _____

EXERCISE 119: Dashes

Add dashes where needed in the following sentences. If a sentence is correct, mark it with a *C* in the left margin.

EXAMPLE: World War I called "the war to end all wars" was, unfortunately, no such thing.

World War I—called "the war to end all wars"—was, unfortunately, no such thing.

1. Tulips, daffodils, hyacinths, lilies all of these flowers grow from bulbs.

2. St. Kitts and Nevis two tiny island nations are now independent after 360 years of British rule.

3. "But it's not" She paused and reconsidered her next words.

4. He considered several different majors history, English, political science, and business before deciding on journalism.

5. The two words added to the Pledge of Allegiance in the 1950s "under God" remain part of the Pledge today.

NAME _____ DATE _____ SCORE _____

EXERCISE 120: Parentheses

Add parentheses where necessary in the following sentences. If a sentence is correct, mark it with a *C* in the left margin.

EXAMPLE: The greatest battle of the War of 1812 the Battle of New Orleans was fought after the war was declared over.

The greatest battle of the War of 1812 (the Battle of New Orleans) was fought after the war was declared over.

1. George Orwell's *1984* 1949 focuses on the dangers of a totalitarian society.

2. The final score 45-0 was a devastating blow for the Eagles.

3. Belize formerly British Honduras is a country in Central America.

4. The first phonics book *Phonics Is Fun* has a light blue cover.

5. Some high school students have so many extracurricular activities band, sports, drama club, and school newspaper, for instance that they have little time to study.

NAME _____ DATE _____ SCORE _____

EXERCISE 121: Ellipses

Read this paragraph and follow the instructions below it, taking care in each case not to delete essential information. Write in the spaces provided.

> The most important thing about research is to know when to stop. How does one recognize the moment? When I was eighteen or thereabouts, my mother told me that when out with a young man I should always leave a half-hour before I wanted to. Although I was not sure how this might be accomplished, I recognized the advice as sound, and exactly the same rule applies to research. One must stop *before* one has finished; otherwise, one will never stop and never finish. (Barbara Tuchman, *Practicing History*)

1. Delete a phrase from the middle of one sentence and mark the omission with ellipses.

2. Delete words at the beginning of any sentence and mark the omission with ellipses.

NAME _____ DATE _____ SCORE _____

3. Delete words at the end of any sentence and mark the omission with ellipses.

4. Delete one complete sentence from the middle of the passage and mark the omission with ellipses.

NAME _____ DATE _____ SCORE _____

EXERCISE 122: Review of Colons, Dashes, Parentheses, Brackets, Slashes

Add appropriate punctuation—colons, dashes, parentheses, brackets, or slashes—to the following sentences. Be prepared to explain why you chose the punctuation marks you did. Write your changes in or between the lines. If a sentence is correct, mark it with a *C* in the left margin.

EXAMPLE: There was one thing she was sure of if she did well at the interview, the job would be hers.

There was one thing she was sure of: If she did well at the interview, the job would be hers.

1. Mark Twain Samuel L. Clemens made the following statement "I can live for two months on a good compliment."

2. Liza Minnelli, the actress singer who starred in several films, is the daughter of Judy Garland.

3. Saudi Arabia, Oman, Yemen, Qatar, and the United Arab Emirates all these are located on the Arabian Peninsula.

4. John Adams 1735-1826 was the second president of the United States; John Quincy Adams 1767-1848 was the sixth.

5. The sign said "No tresspassing *sic*."

NAME _____ DATE _____ SCORE _____

6. *Checkmate* a term derived from the Persian phrase meaning "the king is dead" announces victory in chess.

7. The following people were present at the meeting the president of the board of trustees, three trustees, and twenty reporters.

8. Before the introduction of the potato in Europe, the parsnip was a major source of carbohydrates in fact, it was a dietary staple.

9. In this well-researched book (*Crime Movies* New York Norton, 1980), Carlos Clarens studies the gangster genre in film.

10. I remember reading though I can't remember where that Upton Sinclair sold plots to Jack London.

NAME _____ DATE _____ SCORE _____

EXERCISE 123: *ie* or *ei*

Fill in the blanks with the proper *ie* or *ei* combination. After completing the exercise, use your dictionary to check your answers.

EXAMPLE: conc_ei_ve

1. rec____pt
2. var____ty
3. caff____ne
4. ach____ve
5. kal____doscope
6. misch____f
7. effic____nt
8. v____n
9. spec____s
10. suffic____nt

NAME _____ DATE _____ SCORE _____

EXERCISE 124: Suffixes

Combine the following words with the suffixes in parentheses. Determine whether to keep or drop the silent *e*; be prepared to explain your choice.

EXAMPLE: fate (al)
fatal

1. surprise (ing)

2. sure (ly)

3. force (ible)

4. manage (able)

5. due (ly)

6. outrage (ous)

7. service (able)

8. awe (ful)

9. shame (ing)

10. shame (less)

NAME _____ DATE _____ SCORE _____

EXERCISE 125: Final *y*

Add the endings in parentheses to the following words. Change or keep the final *y* as you see fit; be prepared to explain your choice.

EXAMPLE: party (ing)

        partying

1. journey (ing)

2. study (ed)

3. carry (ing)

4. shy (ly)

5. study (ing)

6. sturdy (ness)

7. merry (ment)

8. likely (hood)

9. plenty (ful)

10. supply (er)

NAME _____ DATE _____ SCORE _____

EXERCISE 126: Capitalization

Capitalize words where necessary in these sentences. Write your changes in or between the lines.

EXAMPLE: John F. Kennedy won the pulitzer prize for his book *profiles in courage*.

John F. Kennedy won the ᴾpulitzer ᴾprize for his ᴾprofiles in ᶜcourage.

1. The brontë sisters wrote *jane eyre* and *wuthering heights*, two nineteenth-century novels that are required reading in many english classes that study victorian literature.

2. It was a beautiful day in the spring—it was april 15, to be exact—but all Ted could think about was the check he had to write to the internal revenue service and the bills he had to pay by friday.

3. Traveling north, they hiked through british columbia, planning a leisurely return on the cruise ship *canadian princess*.

Copyright © 1998 by Harcourt Brace & Company. All rights reserved.

NAME _____ DATE _____ SCORE _____

4. Alice liked her mom's apple pie better than aunt nellie's rhubarb pie; but she liked grandpa's punch best of all.

5. A new elective, political science 30, covers the vietnam war from the gulf of tonkin to the fall of saigon, including the roles of ho chi minh, the viet cong, and the buddhist monks; the positions of presidents johnson and nixon; and the influence of groups like the student mobilization committee and vietnam veterans against the war.

6. When the central high school drama club put on a production of shaw's *pygmalion*, the director xeroxed extra copies of the parts for eliza doolittle and professor henry higgins so he could give them to the understudies.

NAME _____ DATE _____ SCORE _____

7. Shaking all over, Bill admitted, "driving on the los angeles freeway is a frightening experience for a kid from the bronx, even in a bmw."

8. The new united federation of teachers contract guarantees teachers many paid holidays, including columbus day, veterans day, and washington's birthday; a week each at christmas and easter; and two full months (july and august) in the summer.

9. The sociology syllabus included the books *beyond the best interests of the child, regulating the poor,* and *a welfare mother;* in anthropology we were to begin by studying the stone age; and in geology we were to focus on the mesozoic era.

10. Winners of the nobel peace prize include lech walesa, former leader of the polish trade union solidarity; the reverend dr. martin luther king, jr., founder of the southern christian leadership conference; and bishop desmond tutu of south africa.

NAME _____ DATE _____ SCORE _____

EXERCISE 127: Italics

Underline to indicate italics where necessary, and delete any italics that are incorrectly used. If a sentence is correct, mark it with a *C* in the left margin.

EXAMPLE: However is a conjunctive adverb, not a coordinating conjunction.

<u>However</u> is a conjunctive adverb, not a coordinating conjunction.

1. I said Carol, not Darryl.

2. A *deus ex machina,* an improbable device used to resolve the plot of a fictional work, is used in Charles Dickens' novel Oliver Twist.

3. He dotted every i and crossed every t.

4. The Metropolitan Opera's production of Carmen was a tour de force for the principal performers.

5. *Laissez-faire* is a doctrine holding that government should not interfere with trade.

6. Antidote and anecdote are often confused because their pronunciations are similar.

7. Hawthorne's novels include Fanshawe, The House of the Seven Gables, The Blithedale Romance, and The Scarlet Letter.

8. Words like mailman, policeman, and fireman are rapidly being replaced by nonsexist terms like letter carrier, police officer, and firefighter.

NAME _____ DATE _____ SCORE _____

9. A classic black tuxedo was considered de rigueur at the charity ball, but Jason preferred to wear his *dashiki*.

10. Thomas Mann's novel Buddenbrooks is a Bildungsroman.

NAME _____ DATE _____ SCORE _____

EXERCISE 128: Hyphens

Divide each of these words into syllables, consulting a dictionary if necessary; then, indicate with a hyphen where you would divide each word at the end of a line.

EXAMPLE:

    underground   un • der • ground

                     under - ground

1. transcendentalism

2. calliope

3. martyr

4. longitude

5. bookkeeper

6. side-splitting

7. markedly

8. amazing

9. unlikely

10. thorough

EXERCISE 129: Hyphens

Form compound adjectives from the following word groups, inserting hyphens where necessary.

EXAMPLE: A contract for three years

a three-year contract

1. a relative who has long been lost
2. someone who is addicted to video games
3. a salesperson who goes from door to door
4. a display calculated to catch the eye
5. friends who are dearly beloved
6. a household that is centered on a child
7. a line of reasoning that is hard to follow
8. the border between New York and New Jersey
9. a candidate who is thirty-two years old
10. a computer that is friendly to its users

NAME _____ DATE _____ SCORE _____

EXERCISE 130: Hyphens

Add hyphens to the compounds in these sentences wherever they are required. Consult a dictionary if necessary.

EXAMPLE: Alaska was the forty ninth state to join the United States.

   Alaska was the forty-ninth state to join the United States.

1. One of the restaurant's blue plate specials is chicken fried steak.

2. Virginia and Texas are both right to work states.

3. He stood on tiptoe to see the near perfect statue, which was well hidden by the security fence.

4. The five and ten cent store had a self service makeup counter and stocked many up to the minute gadgets.

5. The so called Saturday night special is opposed by pro gun control groups.

6. He ordered two all beef patties with special sauce, lettuce, cheese, pickles, and onions on a sesame seed bun.

7. The material was extremely thought provoking, but it hardly presented any earth shattering conclusions.

Copyright © 1998 by Harcourt Brace & Company. All rights reserved.

NAME _____ DATE _____ SCORE _____

8. The Dodgers Phillies game was rained out, so the long suffering fans left for home.

9. Bone marrow transplants carry the risk of what is known as a graft vs. host reaction.

10. The state funded child care program was considered a highly desirable alternative to family day care.

NAME _____ DATE _____ SCORE _____

EXERCISE 131: Abbreviations

Correct any incorrectly used abbreviations in the following sentences, assuming that all are intended for an academic audience. Write your changes between the lines. If a sentence is correct, mark it with a *C* in the left margin.

EXAMPLE: *Romeo & Juliet* is a play by Wm. Shakespeare.

   Romeo and Juliet is a play by William Shakespeare.

1. The committee meeting, attended by representatives from Action for Children's Television (ACT) and NOW, Sen. Putnam, & the pres. of ABC, convened at 8 A.M. on Mon. Feb. 24 at the YWCA on Germantown Ave.

2. An econ. prof. was suspended after he encouraged his students to speculate on securities issued by corps. under investigation by the SEC.

NAME _____ DATE _____ SCORE _____

3. Benjamin Spock, the M.D. who wrote *Baby and Child Care*, is a respected dr. known throughout the USA.

4. The FDA banned the use of Red Dye no. 2 in food in 1976, but other food additives are still in use.

5. The Rev. Dr. Martin Luther King, Jr., leader of the S.C.L.C., led the famous Selma, Ala., march.

6. Wm. Golding, a novelist from the U.K., won the Nobel Prize in lit.

7. The adult education center, financed by a major computer corp., offers courses in basic subjects like introductory bio. and tech. writing as well as teaching programming languages, such as PASCAL.

NAME _____ DATE _____ SCORE _____

8. All the bros. in the fraternity agreed to write to Pres. Dexter appealing their disciplinary probation under Ch. 4, Sec. 3, of the IFC constitution.

9. A 4 qt. (i.e., 1 gal.) container is needed to hold the salt solution.

10. According to Prof. Morrison, all those taking the MCATs should bring two sharpened no. 2 pencils to the St. Joseph's University auditorium on Sat.

Copyright © 1998 by Harcourt Brace & Company. All rights reserved.

NAME _____ DATE _____ SCORE _____

EXERCISE 132: Numbers

Revise the use of numbers in these sentences, being sure usage is correct and consistent. Write your changes between the lines. If a sentence uses numbers correctly, mark it with a *C* in the left margin.

EXAMPLE: The Empire State Building is one hundred and two stories high.

   The Empire State Building is 102 stories high.

1. *1984*, a novel by George Orwell, is set in a totalitarian society.

2. The English placement examination included a 30-minute personal-experience essay, a 45-minute expository essay, and a 150-item objective test of grammar and usage.

3. In a control group of two hundred forty-seven patients, almost three out of four suffered serious adverse reactions to the new drug.

Copyright © 1998 by Harcourt Brace & Company. All rights reserved.

NAME _____ DATE _____ SCORE _____

4. Before the Thirteenth Amendment to the Constitution, slaves were counted as 3/5 of a person.

5. The intensive membership drive netted 2,608 new members and additional dues of over 5 thousand dollars.

6. They had only 2 choices: Either they could take the yacht at Pier Fourteen, or they could return home to the penthouse at Twenty-seven Harbor View Drive.

7. The atomic number of lithium is three.

8. Approximately 3 hundred thousand schoolchildren in District 6 were given hearing and vision examinations between May third and June 26.

NAME _____ DATE _____ SCORE _____

9. The United States was drawn into the war by the Japanese attack on Pearl Harbor on December seventh, 1941.

10. An upper-middle-class family can spend over 250,000 dollars to raise each child up to age 18.

NAME _____ DATE _____ SCORE _____

EXERCISE 133: Time Management

The following schedule will not only give you an overview of the research process but will also help you manage your time.

Activity	Date Due	Date Completed
Choosing a Topic	_____	_____
Focusing on a Research Question	_____	_____
Doing Exploratory Research	_____	_____
Assembling a Working Bibliography and Making Bibliography Cards	_____	_____
Doing Focused Research and Taking Notes	_____	_____
Outlining	_____	_____
Drafting	_____	_____
Revising	_____	_____
Preparing a Final Draft	_____	_____

NAME _____ DATE _____ SCORE _____

EXERCISE 134: Discovering Your Research Question

1. List five subjects you want to know more about.

2. Which of these subjects would be most interesting for you to do research and write about? Why?

3. Which of these subjects would be most interesting for your audience to read about? Why?

4. Which of these subjects lends itself best to the assignment you have been given? How?

NAME _____ DATE _____ SCORE _____

5. For which of these subjects would you be able to locate the best source material?

6. Which subject do you choose? Why?

7. In the form of a question, state what you hope to find out by doing research and writing about this subject.

NAME _____ DATE _____ SCORE _____

EXERCISE 135: Exploring Your Topic and Locating Sources

1. List the reference books, bibliographies, periodicals, indexes, databases, and other resources that are related to your subject and available to you. Add to this list as you make discoveries in the course of your research and writing. Be sure to record all the information you will need for documenting your sources.

2. Search these resources. List the books, articles, people, organizations, and other material that you think will be most useful to you. Write a brief note to help you remember what you hope to learn or gain from each source. What do you expect each source to contribute to your research and/or your paper? Revise this list as you continue to locate and evaluate source material. (See Exercises 136-139.) Be sure to record all the information you will need for documenting your sources.

NAME _____ DATE _____ SCORE _____

EXERCISE 136: Evaluating Sources

Choose a book, essay, or newspaper/magazine/journal article and analyze its use of source materials.

1. What types of materials are used?

2. Does the writer use more direct quotations than paraphrases? Why?

3. How does the writer give the reader a sense of the source's validity or credibility?

NAME _____ DATE _____ SCORE _____

EXERCISE 137: Locating and Evaluating Sources on the Web Using URL's

Click on the Open button at the top of the Netscape screen. Enter one of the URL's listed at the end of Chapter 33 in *The Brief Holt Handbook*. Answer the following questions. (Your answers will vary.) Also, print at least the first page of the document.

1. Is there a Table of Contents (or a list of contents) that tells you the general topics in this document? If so, what are the general topics?

2. Is there an overview of the contents and purpose of the document? If so, what is the purpose of the document?

3. Who is the author? (An author may be a person, people, or an institution.)

4. Does the site provide a "Last Updated" date? What is it?

5. Do graphics interfere with the content or are they appropriately used?

6. Select highlighted text and begin browsing through the site. Is it easy to move around? Do you understand how the site is organized?

NAME _____ DATE _____ SCORE _____

EXERCISE 138: Locating and Evaluating Sources on the Web Using a Key Word Search

Using your own browser and search engine, do the following:

1. Type in: sports medicine

    a. How many documents are found?

    b. How are the listed documents sorted? (usually by relevance or site)

    c. Are any of the listed documents commercial? Are they basically advertisements for a business, clinic, or physician? If so, how many?

    d. Are any of the listed documents unrelated to sports medicine? How many?

2. Type in: sports+ medicine+ college (Excite on Netscape uses + signs; your browser and search engine may vary. Check the section on Search Tips.)

    a. How many documents are found?

    b. If you wanted to locate documents about all athletes and sports medicine, what might you use for your key word search?

    c. Select one document, and browse through it. Print at least the first page of this document.

NAME _____ DATE _____ SCORE _____

EXERCISE 139: Doing Your Own Key Word Search

Type in your own key word search on a topic of your choosing, revising the key words as necessary to obtain a manageable list of documents. Select one document, and answer these questions. Print at least the first page of the document.

1. What is the source of the information?

2. Is this document an advertisement or other commercial pitch? If so, what is being sold?

3. Who is the author (sponsoring institution)? What makes this author credible and reliable (or not)?

4. Is the "Last Updated" date provided? What is it?

5. Does the text adhere to the conventions of research material that would be expected from print material? If yes, briefly describe how the document meets those conventions. If no, what is lacking?

6. Briefly evaluate the graphics, sound, or video. Are they used to enhance the text, or do they mask a lack of solid content?

NAME _____ DATE _____ SCORE _____

EXERCISE 140: Citing Electronic Sources

Use proper documentation format for electronic sources to cite the following sources.

1. Cite the source you used in Exercise 137: Locating and Evaluating Sources on the Web Using URL's.

2. Cite one source you located in Exercise 138: Locating and Evaluating Sources on the Web Using a Key Word Search.

3. Cite the source you used in Exercise 139: Doing Your Own Key Word Search.

NAME _____ DATE _____ SCORE _____

EXERCISE 141: Summarizing

Assume that in preparation for a paper on "the rise of suburbia," you read the following passage from the book *Great Expectations: America and the Baby Boom Generation* by Landon Y. Jones (New York: Ballantine, 1986). Reread the passage and then write a brief summary.

> As an internal migration, the settling of the suburbs was phenomenal. In the twenty years from 1950 to 1970, the population of the suburbs doubled from 36 million to 72 million. No less than 83 percent of the total population growth in the United States during the 1950s was in the suburbs, which were growing fifteen times faster than any other segment of the country. As people packed and moved, the national mobility rate leaped by 50 percent. The only other comparable influx was the wave of European immigrants to the United States around the turn of the century. But as *Fortune* pointed out, more people moved to the suburbs every year than had ever arrived on Ellis Island.
>
> By now, bulldozers were churning up dust storms as they cleared the land for housing developments. More than a million acres of farmland were plowed under every year during the 1950s. Millions of apartment-dwelling parents with two children were suddenly realizing that two children could be doubled up in a spare bedroom, but a third child cried loudly for something more. The proportion of new houses with three or more bedrooms, in fact, rose from one-third in 1947 to three-quarters in 1954. The necessary *Lebensraum* could only be found in the suburbs. There was a housing

NAME _____ DATE _____ SCORE _____

shortage, but young couples armed with VA and FHA loans built their dream homes with easy credit and free spending habits that were unthinkable to the baby-boom grandparents, who shook their heads with the Depression still fresh in their memories. Of the 13 million homes built in the decade before 1958, 11 million of them—or 85 percent—were built in the suburbs. Home ownership rose 50 percent between 1940 and 1950, and another 50 percent by 1960. By then, one-fourth of *all* housing in the United States had been built in the fifties. For the first time, more Americans owned homes than rented them.

We were becoming a land of gigantic nurseries. The biggest were built by Abraham Levitt, the son of poor Russian-Jewish immigrants, who had originally built houses for the Navy during the war. The first of three East Coast Levittowns went up on the potato fields of Long Island. Exactly $7900—or $60 a month and no money down—bought you a Monopoly-board bungalow with four rooms, attic, washing machine, outdoor barbecue, and a television set built into the wall. The 17,447 units eventually became home to 82,000 people, many of whom were pregnant or wanted to be. In a typical story on the suburban explosion, one magazine breathlessly described a volleyball game of nine couples in which no less than five of the women were expecting.

NAME _____ DATE _____ SCORE _____

EXERCISE 142: Paraphrasing

Paraphrase one paragraph of the passage from Landon Y. Jones' book *Great Expectations* that appears in Exercise 141.

EXERCISE 143: Quoting

Write a paragraph for a paper on "the rise of suburbia" that combines summary, paraphrase, and quotation of the passage from Jones that appears in Exercise 141. Be prepared to explain why you used summary, paraphrase, and quotation as you did.

EXERCISE 144: Documentation

1. Insert the necessary MLA-style parenthetical citation(s) of source material into the paragraph you wrote for Exercise 143. Publication information for the Jones book appears in Exercise 141. Assume that the page number you need to refer to is 27.

2. In the space below, write the entry you would use for the Jones book on your MLA-style Works Cited page.